D1116125

Between Deterrence
and Détente

Between Deterrence and Détente

British Ambassador Sir Roger Makins' Perspective on US Foreign Policy in 1953

Jeffrey LaMonica

To the Chief!

2020

LEXINGTON BOOKS

Lanham • Boulder • New York • London

Published by Lexington Books
An imprint of The Rowman & Littlefield Publishing Group, Inc.
4501 Forbes Boulevard, Suite 200, Lanham, Maryland 20706
www.rowman.com

6 Tinworth Street, London SE11 5AL, United Kingdom

Copyright © 2020 The Rowman & Littlefield Publishing Group, Inc.

All rights reserved. No part of this book may be reproduced in any form or by
any electronic or mechanical means, including information storage and retrieval
systems, without written permission from the publisher, except by a reviewer who
may quote passages in a review.

British Library Cataloguing in Publication Information Available

Library of Congress Cataloging-in-Publication Data

Names: LaMonica, Jeffrey, author.
Title: Between deterrence and détente : British ambassador Sir Roger
    Makins' perspective on US foreign policy in 1953 / Jeffrey LaMonica.
Description: Lanham : Lexington Books, [2020] | Includes bibliographical
    references and index. | Summary: "This book presents a new perspective
    on the Cold War from British Ambassador to the US, Sir Roger Makins,
    during the pivotal year of 1953. The book's primary focus is on the
    historical origins of US diplomacy, a consideration often neglected by
    those who analyze global events and develop foreign policy in the 21st
    century."-- Provided by publisher.
Identifiers: LCCN 2019052541 (print) | LCCN 2019052542 (ebook) | ISBN
    9781793609687 (cloth : alk. paper) | ISBN 9781793609694 (electronic)
Subjects: LCSH: United States--Foreign relations--1953-1961. | Great
    Britain--Foreign relations--1945-1964. | Sherfield, Roger Mellor Makins,
    Baron, 1904-1996. | Cold War.
Classification: LCC E744 .L276 2020 (print) | LCC E744 (ebook) | DDC
    327.73009/04--dc23
LC record available at https://lccn.loc.gov/2019052541
LC ebook record available at https://lccn.loc.gov/2019052542

♾™ The paper used in this publication meets the minimum requirements of
American National Standard for Information Sciences—Permanence of Paper
for Printed Library Materials, ANSI/NISO Z39.48-1992.

To My Mother

Contents

Introduction

US Foreign Affairs and Ambassador Makins in 1953

The year 1953 represented a pivotal moment in the Cold War and set the course of global affairs for the next sixty-five years. The cessation of hostilities in the Korean War resulted in the creation of two opposing countries separated by a contentious demilitarized zone. At the same time, the United States moved toward a policy of coexistence with the People's Republic of China. The Vietminh's struggle against French imperialism in Indochina began its evolution into the US's fifteen-year military entanglement in Vietnam. The recent formation of the United Nations (UN), North Atlantic Treaty Organization (NATO), and the abortive European Defense Community (EDC), gave rise to aspirations for both collective security and a global balance of power. The world's growing appreciation for the destructive potential of atomic technology provided the impetus for international agreements concerning the nonproliferation of weapons of mass destruction.

Great Britain's ambassador to the United States, Sir Roger Makins, provided the British Foreign Office in London with weekly summaries of American political and diplomatic affairs throughout 1953. Examining the events of this critical year through the eyes of this British diplomat provides a fresh perspective on familiar Cold War themes, such as the end of the Korean War, US/China relations, the conflict in Southeast Asia, and the nuclear arms race. Makins was a seasoned diplomat and experienced public figure by 1953. His friendly demeanor made him a favorite among Washington, DC journalists and television reporters. Ambassador Makins had a professional and personal relationship with Dwight D. Eisenhower stretching back to the Second World War, when he served as one of Eisenhower's political advisors. This gave him considerable access to the White House during Eisenhower's presidency. The ambassador was also quick to forge a friendship with Eisenhower's secretary of state, John F. Dulles. This gave Makins a stronger connection with the United States State Department than British Prime Minister Winston Churchill, who despised and mistrusted Dulles. Churchill considered Dulles a bad influence on the President and once described him as "clever enough to be stupid on a rather large scale."[1] Makins possessed a very different attitude toward the Eisenhower/Dulles relationship. The ambassador saw the secretary of State as the more outwardly assertive of the two, but never doubted that it was Eisenhower who had the final word on all matters.[2]

Ambassador Makins was an unwavering advocate for Great Britain's best interests, but also maintained a realistic view of the Anglo-American relationship. International Relations Historian Saul Kelly aptly described Makins as a "transatlantic diplomat" who was always mindful of the nuanced objectives and idiosyncratic personalities of both countries and their leaders. Where Prime Minister Churchill would often place tremendous confidence in the "special relationship" between Great Britain and the United States, only to find himself disappointed and frustrated when American policy diverged from his own, Makins never lost sight of the fact that close ties did not guarantee consensus. The ambassador considered the so-called "special relationship" between Great Britain and the United States to be "a good deal of nonsense." He acknowledged "a special relationship between the United States and Great Britain . . . based on our common language, our common literature, our common goals, our common origins, and our social contacts," but maintained that view within the context of many "special relationships" shared by nations around the world.[3]

Ambassador Makins published a retrospective article in *Foreign Affairs* in October 1954. The essay was an overview of international affairs since the Second World War with a focus on the events of 1953. Makins considered the death of Soviet Premier Joseph Stalin and the proliferation of weapons of mass destruction in 1953 as the beginning of a "third phase" in the post-WWII era, the "first phase" being the 1947 breakup of the wartime alliance that defeated Nazi Germany, and the "second phase" being the polarization of the West versus global communism by 1950. The ambassador believed that the end of Stalin represented the beginning of "an easing on the surface of Soviet relations" with the West. At the same time, the expansion of atomic weapons capabilities created a world where "some careless firecracker could precipitate . . . a holocaust from thermonuclear weapons."[4]

Most of the geopolitical affairs of 1953 still resonate across the international landscape in the early twenty-first century. North and South Korea remain in a state of conflict with little hope of reunification. North Korea's development of a nuclear arsenal has only intensified this crisis. US/China relations continue to resemble a delicate balance between tolerance, cooperation, and tension. The United States and international organizations and alliances, such as the UN, European Union (EU), and NATO, continue to search for peaceful solutions to the spread of Russian influence in places like the Ukraine and Syria, and work to prevent nuclear proliferation.

NOTES

1. John Colville, *The Fringes of Power: 10 Downing Street Diaries, 1939–1955.* (London: W.W. Norton and Co., 1985), 685.

2. Richard Wevill, *Diplomacy, Roger Makins, and the Anglo-American Relationship*, (Burlington, VT: Ashgate, 2014), 102–05; Saul Kelly, "Transatlantic Diplomat: Sir Roger Makins, Ambassador to Washington and Joint Permanent Secretary to the Treasury," *Contemporary British History* (Volume 13, Number 2, 1999): 157–58.

3. Theodore A. Wilson, "Oral History Interview with Sir Roger Makins, 10 August 1970," https://www.trumanlibrary.gov/library/oral-histories/makinsr2; Kelly, 157.

4. Roger Makins, "The World Since the War: The Third Phase," *Foreign Affairs* (33:1 October 1954): 1; ibid., 3; ibid., 7; ibid., 16; ibid; Philip C. Brooks, "Oral History Interview with Sir Roger Makins, 15 June 1964," https://www.trumanlibrary.gov/library/oral-histories/makinsr.

Chapter One

1953 and the Search for an End to the Korean War

General Nam Il of the North Korean Army and US Navy Vice Admiral Charles T. Joy opened truce negotiations in Kaesong, North Korea in July 1951. After agreeing to the establishment of a demilitarized zone between North and South Korea along the 38th Parallel, the meeting broke down due to mutual suspicions, accusations, and stubborn pride on both sides. When the talks eventually resumed in October in Panmunjom, a small town along the neutral demilitarized zone, the main point of contention was the repatriation of prisoners of war. The Americans insisted that North Korean and Chinese prisoners (approximately 170,000) be allowed to choose whether or not they wanted to return to their communist homelands. The North Korean and Chinese delegations rejected this stipulation. The United States commission also demanded information pertaining to thousands of American prisoners who had died from disease and maltreatment while being held captive by the Chinese. Meanwhile, South Korean President Syngman Rhee opposed the armistice altogether and preferred to continue fighting to unify the peninsula.

Militarily, the conflict had degenerated into a stalemate along the 38th Parallel by 1953. Combat resembled the trench warfare of the Great War, with patrols, raids, and small-scale attacks and counterattacks. The US Eighth Army fought against Chinese and North Korean forces over limited territorial objectives, such as "Old Baldy" (Hill, 266) and "Pork Chop Hill." At the same time, President Eisenhower and Secretary of State Dulles attempted to speed up negotiations in Panmunjom by intensifying aerial and naval bombardments against North Korean cities and infrastructure. Threats of an American nuclear attack against North Korea also loomed over the armistice discussions. Prisoner exchanges took place in the spring and summer of 1953 with Operations Little Switch and Big Switch. Over twenty-two thousand North Korean and Chinese prisoners of war chose not to return home. The

5

United States, UN, China, and North Korea finally signed an armistice on July 25, 1953. President Rhee's South Korean government refused to acknowledge the agreement.[1]

Ambassador Makins' weekly political summaries to the British Foreign Office in 1953 chronicle the United States government's waxing and waning prospects for a resolution in Korea, fluctuating American public opinion concerning the conflict, and South Korea's persistent opposition to a negotiated peace. The year started with Prime Minister Churchill causing a minor uproar in the United States by referring to the military situation in Korea as "not bad" and claiming "there are worse things than stalemate."[2] Great Britain's recognition of Communist China and business dealings with the Chinese had already been a strain on Anglo-American relations since 1950. Makins reported on several reactions to the prime minister's remarks, accusing Churchill of being insensitive to and dismissive of the American lives being lost to save South Korea. For example, American radio personality Elmer Davis stated that the British "don't seem to care if it (the conflict in Korea) never ended at all."[3] The prime minister defended his comments in a speech to the House of Commons, "the United States . . . has borne nineteen-twentieths of the burden in blood and treasure . . . but . . . it is our duty . . . to express our opinion frankly and plainly."[4]

In his farewell address on January 15, 1953, President Harry S. Truman stood by his 1950 decision to launch a United States military intervention in Korea. He asserted that the United States and UN saved South Korea from suffering the same fate as countries who had succumbed to Nazi German and Imperial Japanese aggression in the 1930s. President Eisenhower echoed Truman's sentiments in his inaugural address five days later when he proclaimed that the United States's role in Korea was to fight for "freedom" and "light" over "slavery" and "dark."[5]

Despite the encouraging words from the White House, Makins noted a growing "dissatisfaction" with the military stalemate among the American public. Eisenhower addressed the press' concerns over the intensification of the US bombing campaign in Korea in February. The president assured reporters that there was a thoughtful process behind his decision, "I don't believe in doing these things haphazardly and on an individual and arbitrary basis." When asked if it was "right" for President Truman to take action in Korea in the first place, Eisenhower dodged the question with, "That all took place before I came to this office." In response to an inquiry about the ability of the South Korean Army to defend their country without American military support, the president said that the United States and UN could not "remove" themselves from the peninsula so long as a "dangerous situation" persisted there.[6] Makins' February 21 summary to London included Gallup

Poll statistics showing only thirty-eight percent of Americans confident in the president's ability to find a satisfactory solution in Korea.[7]

Makins observed another dip in popular opinion in April, when Chinese forces captured Old Baldy and newspaper coverage of Operation Little Switch revealed the abysmal condition of American prisoners. He described an atmosphere of "emotional instability," "dismay," and "disillusionment" and explained how "the public is horrified by" the poor physical health of the American captives. British Consul to the United States Alastair G. Maitland provided his own assessment of the situation, "American parents, wives, and mothers . . . want their men home safely."[8]

The ambassador took a more optimistic tone later in April, as Operation Little Switch had "raised hopes" in the United States for the possibility of a truce with the Chinese and North Koreans. Makins also reported on an embarrassing miscommunication concerning US policy in Korea between Secretary Dulles and President Eisenhower. On April 6, Dulles told the press that the United States was willing to accept a permanent division of Korea along the 38th Parallel. Eisenhower was quick to "publicly disavowed" Dulles's statement in an address to the American people on ten days later. His speech called for an "honorable armistice," including "free elections in a united Korea." Ambassador Makins called the president's address a "sharp contrast to Mr. Dulles' exploratory reference last week to a division at the waist of Korea."[9]

Prime Minister Churchill spoke about the situation in Korea in the House of Commons in May. Churchill doubted the possibility of "any agreement at the present time on a united Korea." He stated, "I should be very content with even a truce or a cease-fire for the moment."[10] Former Prime Minister Clement R. Attlee kept the Korean conversation going in the House of Commons for the next several days. He expressed concern over American intentions in Korea, "there are elements in the United States that do not want a settlement . . . people who want an all-out war with China and against Communism in general." Attlee also questioned the United States's level of influence over negotiations in Panmunjom, "it would be well if there were other advisers from other United Nations States . . . further settlement should not be left exclusively in American hands."[11] Attlee's critique caused another outrage in the American press. Makins described how the "speech blew up the fire" and the "prevailing sentiment" in the United States was "that the Chinese Communist are unreasonable and perfidious negotiators" and "any hint of criticism" of the American delegation in Panmunjom "by a foreigner is regarded as high treason."[12]

In late May, Makins reported on South Korean opposition to the pending armistice and "their insistence on Korean unity." The ambassador feared that

President Rhee's goal of the unconditional reunification of Korea would go beyond the US/UN mandate to merely "restore peace" on the peninsula and result in an "all out war" with China.[13] President Eisenhower attempted to ease South Korea's concerns over a negotiated peace during a May press conference, "we certainly should never adopt a solution that at least our own conscious tells us is unfair to South Korea."[14] Makins reported that some American "commentators" and "disgruntled members of Congress" sympathized with President Rhee's government and accused Eisenhower of "letting them down" and conceding too much to the communists by settling for a divided Korea. He saw President Rhee as a "rallying point" for Americans who viewed "an armistice which leaves Korea divided" as "a defeat for the United Nations and, worse, for the United States."[15] Furthermore, there was some concern in the United States that a truce in Korea would open the door for international "recognition of Communist China and its admission to the United Nations." Makins claimed, "While a truce will be welcome as putting an end to the hostilities, it will not be regarded as a victory for American policy."[16]

In June, Makins was relieved to inform the Foreign Office that "President Syngman Rhee's continued refusal to endorse the armistice terms is not considered to be an insurmountable obstacle" in the United States and American support for "continuing the war until Korea is united is . . . limited to a very small jingoistic minority."[17] Nevertheless, President Rhee released North Korean prisoners without US/UN approval on June 18. Rhee hoped that this gesture would disrupt armistice talks by removing prisoner of war exchange as a bargaining chip. Consul Maitland was confident that President Rhee's "headstrong behavior" had little effect on negotiations in Panmunjom and only served to test US/UN patience with the South Korean government. Maitland reassured London that "Hope of a truce in Korea has not been abandoned."[18]

Ambassador Makins was confident that "an armistice will shortly be concluded" in early July. He was less optimistic about his prediction seven days later when a "large-scale" Chinese attack on Pork Chop Hill "all but dispelled last week's hopes that a truce was imminent." Nevertheless, President Eisenhower dismissed the Department of Defense's recommendation to retaliate with a "full-scale offensive" and authorized the American delegates in Panmunjom to sign the armistice on July 27.[19]

As he had anticipated, Makins noted a bittersweet climate in the United States after the armistice signing, "There were no celebrations when the news was received. Failure to win a clear cut victory . . . has wounded national pride." He told the Foreign Office that although Eisenhower and Dulles claimed that their "primary task . . . is to unify Korea; . . . Almost no one believes that this can be achieved." The ambassador believed that the established demilitarized zone already laid the foundation for a permanently divided Korea. Furthermore, Makins informed London that the United States intended to maintain its military forces on the peninsula, "the President, members of the Cabinet, and Congressional leaders have emphasized that the truce must not lead to any relaxation in the defense program" and "the Director of Selective Service has announced that there will be no change in monthly conscription."[20]

Article III of the armistice arranged for the repatriation of all prisoners of war within sixty days. At the insistence of the United States, this decree did not apply to North Korean and Chinese prisoners who did not want to return to their home countries. In August, Makins detected "growing suspicions" in the United States that "the Chinese hold 3,000 more Americans than they admit."[21] Consul Maitland told London that "the Communists are refusing to repatriate numbers of Americans on trumped up charges that they were 're-actionaries' or 'dangers to peace.'"[22] The United States withheld 250 Chinese and North Korean prisoners in the event they needed to bargain for any remaining American detainees. Tension over the exchange of prisoners would persist for decades, as the United States and China continued to accuse each other of withholding thousands of detainees.

Article II called for both sides to "cease the introduction" of additional military forces into Korea. Makins remarked on the US/UN pledge to uphold this stipulation by "putting the Communists on notice that any further adventures in Korea would be resisted even at the risk of starting World War III."[23] The American "treaty of mutual assistance" with President Rhee gave the United States permission to "maintain troops in Korea" and "provide about one billion dollars for the rehabilitation" of South Korea for four years. The agreement also required Rhee "to take no unilateral action to unite Korea by military means" and made "it abundantly clear to Syngman Rhee that the United States has no intention of resuming the Korean War to assist him in his political aspirations."[24]

In late August, Ambassador Makins observed some lingering American "dissatisfaction" with the armistice proceedings. He noted that many Americans saw "the inclusion of Russia and India" in the Panmunjom negotiations as a "gesture of Red appeasement."[25] Makins alleged that much of the US public saw the Soviet Union "as an aggressor" in Korea and India as a "pro-Communist . . . anti-American neutral." According to the Ambassador, "most people in this country would agree that . . . only the 16 member nations that sent armed forces to Korea and the South Korean Republic have a right to attend the conference." Even Great Britain was under "widespread suspicion" in the United States for its alleged desire to use the armistice negotiations as a springboard for Communist China's admission to the UN, "most Americans

This monument along the demilitarized zone between North and South Korea commemorates the UN nations who helped negotiate the 1953 armistice that ended the Korean War. *Credit*: artapornp.

are convinced that support for any Communist desideratum is evidence of pro-Communist sympathies."[26]

Makins' September 5 report to London covered Secretary Dulles' September 2 speech to the American Legion in St. Louis, Missouri. Dulles dispelled Chinese accusations of the US's self-serving intentions in the Far East, "We seek no pretext for turning Korea into a United States base on the Asia mainland," but only "the peaceful unification of Korean under a representative form of government." The secretary warned that "the United States and the other 15 members of the United Nations" will take military action "if the armistice should be breached by unprovoked Communist aggression."[27] Makins believed that Dulles's hardline "statement goes further than the Administration has yet gone in public."[28] Dulles's speech also defended American objections to India's involvement in the Korean negotiations, noting how "India . . . had preferred not to join with the forces fighting aggression." He alleged that, despite this, the United States still "seeks friendship with India." Finally, the Secretary assured his audience in St. Louis that "all captured personnel . . . shall be returned" to the United States.[29] Makins estimated that the US government was still pressing the Chinese for "an explanation of what became of 944 Americans known to have been prisoners."[30]

The Eisenhower Administration remained optimistic about the reunification of Korea for a few months after the armistice signing. Secretary Dulles spoke at the UN on September 17 and praised its peace keeping effort in Korea, "for the first time in history an international organization was instrumental in actually repelling armed aggression." He assured the UN that "The United States itself seeks no pretext for using Korea as a place for building up a military outpost on the Asian mainland."[31] Makins described Dulles's UN speech as "uniformly well received" and expressed confidence in the US commitment to a "united and free" Korea. At the same time, the Ambassador criticized China's "continued detention . . . of Allied prisoners" and "22,600 anti-communist Chinese and North Koreans" who want to "escape from Communist slavery."[32] US delegate to the UN Dr. Charles W. Mayo asserted in October that "North Korean and Chinese atrocities" against prisoners of war included "germ warfare" experiments on over six thousand detainees. The ambassador believed Mayo's statement reinforced the "American . . . view that the Chinese Communists, far from qualifying for a seat in the UN, should be treated as hostile barbarians." Mayo's report on prisoner atrocities caused Makins to question whether or not "the Communists" were acting "in good faith" in Panmunjom.[33]

By November, Makins noticed a more cautionary tone in Eisenhower and Dulles' statements concerning the reunification of Korea. The president told reporters he "was hopeful about the prospects," but "would hesitate to make

North Korean soldiers guard the demilitarized border at Panmunjom, while South Korean and American troops patrol the opposite side. The blue conference buildings are part of the Joint Security Area (JSA), where meetings between both sides have occurred sporadically since 1953. An official treaty to end the Korean War and unify the two Koreas is still pending. *Credit:* Karsten Jung.

a flat prediction." The secretary was even less optimistic in his press conference, claiming "it was too soon to say" and blaming the "lack of progress" on intentionally sluggish "oriental bargaining tactics."[34]

President Eisenhower adopted Dulles's hardline rhetoric when speaking about Korea at the Bermuda Conference in December. In his meeting with Prime Minister Churchill, the president threatened to "strike back with atomic weapons" if there "was a deliberate breach of the Armistice."[35] He told both Churchill and French Prime Minister Joseph Laniel that "if we were again attacked in Korea we would not merely attempt to hold by using ground troops . . . but we would exert reprisals by attacking" with "a much more intensive scale of warfare" and the "means . . . for delivering atomic weapons."[36] The president's casual talk about unleashing weapons of mass destruction alarmed his British and French counterparts, who considered atomic weapons outside the scope of conventional military options. Churchill attributed Eisenhower's hawkish statements in Bermuda as evidence of Secretary Dulles's "terrible influence" on the president.[37]

The close of 1953 never brought a final peace resolution in Korea. The truce remained strictly a military arrangement providing for the cessation of hostilities, establishment of a demilitarized zone, and exchange of prisoners. Ambassador Makins praised the Korean armistice as a diplomatic success in his 1954 article in *Foreign Affairs*, but cautioned that "it remains to be seen whether an effective halt has yet been called to Communist encroachment in Asia."[38] The armistice recommended that an official peace conference be held between the governments of North and South Korea in order to reunify the country. A meeting of that kind is still pending as of 2020.

NOTES

1. Steven H. Lee, "Korean War (1949–1953)," in *Twentieth-Century War and Conflict: A Concise Encyclopedia*, edited by Gordon Martel (West Sussex, UK: John Wiley and Sons, Ltd., 2015), 119–20; Brad D. Lookingbill, *The American Military: A Narrative History* (West Sussex, UK: John Wiley and Sons, Ltd., 2013), 308–12.

2. Roger Makins, "Weekly Political Summary, 3–9 January 1953."

3. Roger Makins, "Weekly Political Summary, 3–9 January 1953"; Makins, "Weekly Political Summary, 7–13 February 1953."

4. Winston S. Churchill, "Foreign Affairs, House of Commons, 11 May 1953," http://hansard.millbanksystems.com/commons/1953/may/11/foreign-affairs #column_883.

5. Harry S. Truman, "Farewell Address to the American People, 15 January 1953," http://www.presidency.ucsb.edu/ws/index.php?pid=14392; Dwight D. Eisenhower, "Inaugural Address, 20 January 1953," http://www.presidency.ucsb.edu/ws/?pid

=9600; Dwight D. Eisenhower, "Annual Message to the Congress on the State of the Union, 2 February 1953," http://www.presidency.ucsb.edu/ws/?pid=9829.

6. Makins, "Weekly Political Summary, 7–13 February 1953;" Dwight D. Eisenhower, "News Conference, 17 February 1953," http://www.presidency.ucsb.edu/ws/index.php?pid=9623.

7. Makins, "Weekly Political Summary, 14–20 February 1953."

8. Makins, "Weekly Political Summary, 21–27 March 1953;" Makins, "Weekly Political Summary, 18–24 April 1953;" Makins, "Weekly Political Summary, 28–3 April 1953."

9. Makins, "Weekly Political Summary, 4–10 April 1953;" Dwight D. Eisenhower, "Chance for Peace Address, 16 April 1953," https://www.eisenhower.archives .gov/all_about_ike/speeches/chance_for_peace.pdf; Makins, "Weekly Political Summary, 11–17 April 1953."

10. Churchill, "Foreign Affairs, House of Commons, 11 May 1953."

11. Clement R. Attlee, "Foreign Affairs, House of Commons, 12 May 1953," http://hansard.millbanksystems.com/commons/1953/may/12/foreign-affairs #S5CV0515P0_19530512_HOC_263.

12. Makins, "Weekly Political Summary, 9–15 May 1953."

13. Makins, "Weekly Political Summary, 23–29 May 1953."

14. Dwight D. Eisenhower, "News Conference, 28 May 1953," http://www.presi dency.ucsb.edu/ws/index.php?pid=9860.

15. Roger Makins, "Weekly Political Summary, 30 May–5 June 1953."

16. Makins, "Weekly Political Summary, 30 May–5 June 1953."

17. Makins, "Weekly Political Summary, 6–12 June 1953;" Makins, "Weekly Political Summary, 13–19 June 1953;" Makins, "Weekly Political Summary, 20–26 June 1953."

18. Makins, "Weekly Political Summary, 27 June–3 July 1953."

19. Makins, "Weekly Political Summary, 4–10 July 1953."

20. Makins, "Weekly Political Summary, 11–17 July 1953."

21. "Armistice Agreement for the Restoration of the South Korean State, 27 July 1953," https://www.ourdocuments.gov/doc.php?flash=true&doc=85&page=transcr ipt; Makins, "Weekly Political Summary, 25–31 July 1953."

22. Makins, "Weekly Political Summary, 25–31 July 1953."

23. "Armistice Agreement for the Restoration of the South Korean State, 27 July 1953;" Makins, "Weekly Political Summary, 1–7 August 1953."

24. Makins, "Weekly Political Summary, 8–14 August 1953."

25. Ibid.

26. Makins, "Weekly Political Summary, 15–21 August, 1953."

27. John F. Dulles, "Korean Problems, 2 September 1953." https://history.state. gov/historicaldocuments/frus1952-54v13p1/d385.

28. Makins, "Weekly Political Summary, 28 August–4 September 1953."

29. Dulles, "Korean Problems, 2 September 1953."

30. Makins, "Weekly Political Summary, 28 August–4 September 1953."

31. John F. Dulles, "Address to the United Nations, 17 September 1953."

32. Makins, "Weekly Political Summary, 12–18 September 1953."

33. Makins, "Weekly Political Summary, 3–9 October 1953."

34. Makins, "Weekly Political Summary, 31 October–7 November 1953."

35. "Memorandum of Conversation, by the Secretary of State, Bermuda, 4 December 1953," in *Foreign Relations of the United States, 1952–1954, Western European Security, Volume V, Part 2*, https://history.state.gov/historicaldocuments/frus1952-54v05p2/d336.

36. "United States Delegation Minutes, Bermuda, Undated," in *Foreign Relations of the United States, 1952–1954, Western European Security, Volume V, Part 2*, https://history.state.gov/historicaldocuments/frus1952-54v05p2/d353.

37. Lord Moran, *Churchill: Taken from the Diaries of Lord Moran*. (Boston, MA: Houghton Mifflin Co., 1966), 433; ibid., 469; Colville, 662.

38. Makins, "The World Since the War: The Third Phase," 4.

Chapter Two

1953 and the Roots of a Sustainable US/China Relationship

While the United States and Communist China fought on behalf of their respective allies on the Korean Peninsula in 1953, the two nations also took their first steps toward peaceful coexistence. Relations between the two counties had declined steadily since Mao Tse Tung's creation of the People's Republic of China in October 1949. The United States refused to acknowledge Mao as the official leader of China but, instead, recognized Chiang Kai Shek's Republic of China on the island of Taiwan. Furthermore, the United States provided arms and economic aid in support of Chiang's Nationalist regime.

China's relationship with the United States worsened when Mao entered a "friendship" agreement with the Soviet Union in 1950. Soviet Premier Joseph Stalin urged China to assist communist North Korea in its struggle against US-backed South Korea in October of that year. Mao saw Chinese intervention in Korea as a way to block US influence in Asia and spread his brand of communism throughout the region. There were nearly half a million Chinese troops in Korea by the end of 1950. Mao ordered this "volunteer" expeditionary force to sweep all US forces from the Korean Peninsula. When the conflict devolved into a stalemate along the 38th parallel in 1951, US/China relations sank to an all-time low. The commander of US forces, General Douglas MacArthur, believed that waging total war against China itself was the only way to break the deadlock in Korea. He called upon President Harry S. Truman to authorize the aerial bombardment of Chinese cities, a naval blockade of China's coastline, and even the use atomic weapons. The president rejected MacArthur's request to escalate the conflict and ultimately relieved MacArthur of his command. Unfortunately, this did not mitigate the damage to US/Chinese relations. The Chinese would not soon forget MacArthur's plan to annihilate their country.[1]

The Chiang Kai Shek Memorial Hall in Taipei, Taiwan. The US recognized Chiang's Nationalist Chinese government in Taiwan as the official government of China from 1949 until 1979. There are still conflicting opinions in Taiwan, China, and across the international community as to whether or not there are two Chinas or one. *Credit:* fishwork.

It was in the wake of these contentious events that British Ambassador to the United States Sir Roger Makins reported to London about US policy toward China in 1953. The new administration in the White House immediately went to work establishing a policy that included both pressure and tolerance toward China. Newly elected President Dwight D. Eisenhower removed the United States Navy's Seventh Fleet from the Taiwan Strait in February. This withdrawal of US vessels represented a threat to China, as President Truman had ordered the Seventh into the strait in 1950 to discourage Chiang's Nationalists in Taiwan from using military force against Communist China. With the United States Navy gone, Chiang's military had an open sea lane for invading the Chinese mainland. In a message to Congress, President Eisenhower asserted that "the Seventh Fleet no longer be employed to shield Communist China." When asked about using nuclear weapons against China in a press conference, the new president said, "these things" were still "under consideration."[2] While Eisenhower's initial actions and comments seemed to suggest a hardline posture toward China, Makins assured London that the president's China policy was still only in its formative stage. The ambassador observed how the Eisenhower Administration's "no definite plans" stance on China led to some overzealous speculation among American reporters, that "a naval blockade of China has been widely predicted" by a large body of the press.[3]

When reporters probed Eisenhower on his China policy later in February, he expressed signs of restraint. In response to an inquiry about the possibility of an economic embargo or naval blockade against China, the president replied, "There has been no study on it that has been brought up yet to me."[4] Eisenhower's Secretary of State, John F. Dulles, also downplayed the chances of a blockade during his own press conference that month. By the end of February, Makins told London that the media's "excitement and agitation" over Eisenhower's China policy had "died down with remarkable rapidity." He commended "the Administration's efforts to deflate the balloon."[5]

Makins reported to London on US/Chinese relations again in March. This time, he included Gallup Poll results showing sixty-one percent of Americans in favor of "supplying Chiang with warships to blockade and aircraft to bomb Communist China."[6] Despite the public pressure, President Eisenhower made no references to China in his highly publicized "Chance for Peace" speech in April. The ambassador noted this glaring omission in his summary to London that week. He claimed that the president's speech fell "a little short of setting out a bold new policy" regarding Chiang Kai Shek, Taiwan, and China. Meanwhile, Sino/American affairs appeared in the Soviet press.[7] The Russian newspaper *Pravda* recognized Eisenhower's failure to "illuminate" his position on China in his speech and accused American policy in Asia of being "martial" and "aggressive." The article went on to criticize the United

States for not recognizing Mao's China and asserted that the international community "cannot function . . . while Communist China remains outside."[8] American radio news broadcaster Edward R. Murrow also made bold statements favoring US recognition of Communist China. Ambassador Makins regarded these "sensible voices" as cries "in the wilderness" of a largely anti-Chinese America.[9]

During the early days of the Eisenhower Presidency, Makins notified London of the budding American animosity toward Great Britain due to its economic and diplomatic relations with the Chinese, "trade with China . . . and our recognition of the Communist regime are being used to beat us." The Ambassador initially dismissed these sentiments as *cliché*, "blame the British is a well-tried recipe in this country."[10] By May, however, Makins referred to Great Britain's economic relationship with China as "one of the most sensitive points in Anglo-American relations." The ambassador's change in attitude was due in part to Assistant Secretary of State for Economic Affairs Harold F. Linder's announcement that the United States "was seeking to tighten the restrictions imposed by its allies on the flow of strategic materials to China." Other political commentators chimed in after Linder's comment went public. *New York Times* Washington, DC, correspondent Arthur Krock demanded "a full embargo on trade with China." Former presidential candidate and future US Ambassador to the UN Adlai Stevenson II was also "highly critical of allied trade with China." Makins claimed that he personally encountered "the sentiment that it is morally indefensible to trade with the enemy . . . everywhere I go in this country."[11]

British politician Clement Attlee defended his country's relationship with China in a controversial speech before the House of Commons on May 12, "We are constantly pressed not to trade with China . . . We cannot survive if we are to be restricted . . . our American friends will recognize this." Attlee also addressed Great Britain's attitude toward China's admission to the UN, "I do not believe that China is a mere puppet in the hands of Russia . . . she will wear her Communism with a difference . . . China should take her rightful place on the Security Council."[12] One of Makins' reports to London pointed out a bit of hypocrisy in US protests against British trade with China, "It may perhaps be embarrassing . . . that the US imported last year from Communist China about $29 million worth of goods. This is far in excess of our own imports from China."[13]

The Ambassador reported on another allegation against Great Britain's dealings with China from Wisconsin Senator Joseph McCarthy in late May. McCarthy accused "British-owned ships" of transporting "Chinese Communist troops along the China coast." Although the American media publicized the Senator's accusation, newspapers also published the Wheelock Marden

Shipping Line's statement refuting his claim. Makins was relieved to inform London that this rare case of balanced reporting prevented McCarthy's statement from turning into a "violent outburst" of American public opinion against Great Britain. For his own part, the ambassador notified the American press that the ships in question "were of Panamanian registry."[14] Makins offered London his own assessment of Senator McCarthy, "It is doubtful whether he has any deep idealistic interest in any of the causes he champions; he appears rather to pursue his course for his own personal ends, regardless of truth or justice."[15] The self-serving motives behind McCarthy's communist witch hunts throughout the 1950s would ultimately led to his loss of credibility and the end of his political career.

Makins did express concern over US threats to leave the UN if the organization admitted Communist China, "American opinion on this subject was illustrated this week in the Senate Appropriations Committee . . . by 20 votes to 3 . . . putting the United States' contribution to the United Nations on a monthly basis subject to automatic cancellation if the Chinese Communists gain a seat."[16] On 28 May, Eisenhower told the American press that "Red Communist China . . . is subservient to Moscow" and, therefore, "should not" be accepted into the UN. When asked about British trade with China, the President made a vague reference to "instances over the past 2 or 3 years where the Communists have been helped by certain kinds of trade," but withheld his own opinion on the matter.[17] Makins closed his summary for May 30, with an assessment of current Anglo-American relations from the British Consul in Los Angeles, California, "never since . . . 1948 have the public in general been so incensed at perfidious Albion."[18]

Tension between the US and Great Britain over relations with China continued into the summer. In June, Makins reported on "a vote of 76 to 0" in the US senate in favor of keeping Communist China out of the UN. He conveyed to London the *Wall Street Journal's* attempt to explain the United States's interpretation of the UN in comparison to the British view, "the United States looks upon the United Nations . . . as an instrument of action, a sort of military alliance, against Communist regimes" while "the United Kingdom sees it as a meeting place."[19] Makins highlighted some improvement in Anglo-American affairs in a July report to London. He reported on how the American press portrayed a recent conference between the United States, British, and French foreign ministers in a positive light and seemed "satisfied that Mr. Dulles has not sold his soul and country" to the British. At the meeting, the British and French ministers agreed not to trade "strategic materials" with the Chinese and decided to curb "the question of admitting Communist China to the United Nations" for "the near future."[20]

Makins' August 1, 1953 report to London observed how the recent truce negotiations in Korea had given rise to some mixed feelings over American recognition of Communist China. On one hand, the US Senate Foreign Relations Committee announced that the Chinese must not be allowed to use the crisis in Korea to "shoot their way into the United Nations." Meanwhile, "more dispassionate commentators" consider China's participation in the negotiations in Panmunjom as "a *de facto* recognition which makes the United States' position on the subject increasingly absurd."[21] The ambassador opined that "there are signs that the attitude towards recognition is becoming less rigid," as some "press reports" speculated "a plan for seating both of the Chinese governments in the United Nations." Nevertheless, American attitudes toward Great Britain's relationship with China remained tense. Makins claimed that most Americans believed "the British position on the question" of Chinese admittance to the UN was fueled by their "indecent haste to resume fuller trade with China."[22]

August brought additional threats to "withdrawal from the UN in the event of attempts to include China" from California Senator and US Senate majority leader William F. Knowland. Vice President Richard M. Nixon also urged "the United States to veto any attempt to admit Red China to the United Nations" at the American Legion Convention in St. Louis in September. September Gallup Poll results showed sixty-eight percent of Americans "against the admission of Communist China to the United Nations."[23] In October, Ambassador Makins lamented that "United States recognition of Communist China, or American acceptance of the Chinese Communists in the United Nations, looks more remote than ever." Recent American suspicions that the Soviet Union was "trying to prevent a meeting between the United States and China" in order to prolong the Korea War fueled Makins' pessimism.[24] Senator McCarthy launched another "emotional attack on British trade with China" in November. McCarthy alleged that "British exports to China increased 1,500 percent between January 1952 and January 1953." Makins feared that this "renewed campaign of vilification on this score might easily arouse bitter feelings towards Britain among large segments of the public."[25]

The Bermuda Conference in December finally allowed President Eisenhower to personally address Anglo/Chinese relations with British Prime Minister Winston Churchill. The president anticipated that Churchill would use the meeting to "plead China's case," so he opened the discussion on December 4 by urging the Prime Minister to align Great Britain's policy with the United States and cutoff all trade with China. Churchill told Eisenhower that it was impossible for Great Britain to terminate its existing economic ties with Communist China, but promised to support the United States in opposing China's admission to the UN.[26] Later in the conference, French Foreign Minister

The mausoleum of Mao Tse Tung in Tiananmen Square in Beijing, China. The Eisenhower Administration spent most of 1953 trying to determine whether or not Mao was a Chinese version of Stalin. It would take decades for the US government to realize that Communist China operated independently from the Soviet Union. *Credit:* ymgerman.

Georges-Augustin Bidault described the French perspective on Communist China's place in the world. He argued that all communist countries were not part of a single united bloc. In fact, he speculated that China's relationship with the Soviet Union was "not as smooth as generally believed." Bidault alluded to the revolving door of Soviet ambassadors to China since 1949 as evidence of discord. Secretary Dulles concurred with Bidault's observation. He saw Mao's unwillingness to be manipulated by Moscow as an opportunity for the United States to divide the two communist superpowers. The secretary proposed two possible methods for driving a wedge between China and the Soviet Union. One involved "being nice" to the Chinese in order to "wean" them from the Soviets. The other employed the application of military, diplomatic, and economic "pressure and strain" to "compel" China away from the Soviet Union. Dulles claimed that British policy represented the former, while he preferred the latter.[27]

Ambassador Makins published a reflective article in *Foreign Affairs* in 1954. His essay expressed optimism regarding China, as he believed that 1953 had revealed that Communist China was "something quite different from an ordinary Soviet satellite." The Eisenhower Administration's patience (or indecision) in defining US posture toward China in 1953 eventually evolved into a stance similar to that of the British. The United States gradually came to realize that Communist China was not just another Soviet Union, but represented "Communist with a difference" as Clement Attlee had observed in 1953.[28] US policy toward China grew into something far more complex than Dulles's 1953 "pressure and strain" proposal as well. For over six decades, US/China affairs have come to include tolerance, economic and diplomatic cooperation, and, at times, "pressure."

NOTES

1. Lookingbill, 302; Gary J. Bjorge, "Chinese Civil War (Modern)," in *Twentieth-Century War and Conflict: A Concise Encyclopedia*, edited by Gordon Martel (West Sussex, UK: John Wiley and Sons, Ltd., 2015), 57.

2. Eisenhower, "Annual Message to the Congress on the State of the Union, 2 February 1953."

3. Makins, "Weekly Political Summary, 7–13 February 1953."

4. Eisenhower, "News Conference, 17 February 1953."

5. Makins, "Weekly Political Summary, 14–20 February 1953;" Makins, "Weekly Political Summary, 21–27 February 1953."

6. Makins, "Weekly Political Summary, 14–20 March 1953."

7. Eisenhower, "Chance for Peace Address, 16 April 1953;" Makins, "Weekly Political Summary, 11–17 April 1953."

8. Central Intelligence Agency, "Summary of *Pravda's* Reply to President Eisenhower's Address of 16 April," (April 25, 1953), https://www.cia.gov/library/readingroom/docs/DOC_0000269307.pdf.

9. Makins, "Weekly Political Summary, 2–8 May 1953."

10. Makins, "Weekly Political Summary, 7–13 February 1953."

11. Makins, "Weekly Political Summary, 2–8 May 1953."

12. Attlee, "Foreign Affairs, House of Commons, 12 May 1953."

13. Makins, "Weekly Political Summary, 16–22 May 1953."

14. ibid.

15. Makins, "Weekly Political Summary, 23–29 May 1953."

16. ibid.

17. Eisenhower, "News Conference, 28 May 1953."

18. Makins, "Weekly Political Summary, 23–29 May 1953."

19. Makins, "Weekly Political Summary, 30 May-5 June 1953."

20. Makins, "Weekly Political Summary, 11–17 July 1953."

21. Makins, "Weekly Political Summary, 25–31 July 1953."

22. Makins, "Weekly Political Summary, 1–7 August 1953."

23. Makins, "Weekly Political Summary, 8–14 August 1953;" Makins, "Weekly Political Summary, 28 August–4 September 1953;" Makins, "Weekly Political Summary, 5–11 September 1953."

24. Makins, "Weekly Political Summary, 25 September–2 October 1953."

25. Makins, "Weekly Political Summary, 7–11 November 1953."

26. "Memorandum of Conversation, by the Secretary of State, Bermuda, 4 December 1953," in *Foreign Relations of the United States, 1952-1954, Western European Security, Volume V, Part 2.*

27. "United States Delegation Minutes, Bermuda, 4 December 1953," in *Foreign Relations of the United States, 1952–1954, Western European Security, Volume V, Part 2*, https://history.state.gov/historicaldocuments/frus1952-54v05p2/d341.

28. Makins, "The World Since the War: The Third Phase," 6.

Chapter Three

Decolonization in 1953

French Indochina, British Malaya, and the Middle East

Imperial possessions in Africa and Asia posed more of a burden than a benefit to European nations in the wake of the Second World War. Countries like Great Britain and France were preoccupied with postwar reconstruction and the possibility of Europe becoming the United States and Soviet Union's Cold War battleground. By the 1950s, decolonization became more of a question of "when and how" than "if." Nevertheless, imperial retrenchment would take decades to unfold in a wide variety of both violent and nonviolent episodes. The United States looked at post-WWII decolonization through the lens of its Cold War "containment" strategy, where all revolutions, civil wars, and independence movements represented opportunities to stop the spread of global communism.

Catholic missionaries from France arrived in Indochina (Vietnam, Cambodia, and Laos) in the late 1700s. France gradually increased its military, economic, and political influence over the region until Indochina became a French protectorate by the end of the nineteenth century. France temporarily lost its claim over Indochina during the Second World War, when Imperial Japanese forces occupied it from 1940 until 1945. The 1945 Declaration of Indochina increased Indochinese autonomy after Imperial Japan's surrender, but also reinstated French authority. At the same time, Vietnamese nationalist leader and communist Ho Chi Minh declared an independent Democratic Republic of Vietnam (DRV). The 1946 March Accords settled the dispute by partitioning Indochina into Laos, Cambodia, and a temporarily divided Vietnam. The DRV existed north of the 16th Parallel while the French controlled the south. Armed conflict erupted between the French and Ho's DRV when negotiations to unify the country broke down in December 1946. The French created an anti-communist South Vietnamese army and government under Emperor Bao Dai in 1950. The United States provided funds for the French war effort while the Soviet Union and Communist China financed the DRV. Combat was a mix of conventional battles and guerilla warfare, which spilled over into neighboring Cambodia and Laos, and claiming over a half of a million lives. The French shifted their strategic goal in 1953 from defeating the DRV to forcing a negotiated peace.[1]

Similar to the French in Indochina, British influence in Malaya began in the late 1700s and intensified through the nineteen century. The Japanese occupied most of the peninsula during the Second World War until the British resumed control over the Malayan Union in 1946. The nationalist Malayan Communist Party and its Malayan National Liberation Army (MNLA) had fought against Japanese occupation during the Second World War and rose up against the British in 1948. Numbering less than ten thousand troops, the small liberation army waged unconventional *guerilla* warfare against the British in the jungles and mountains across the peninsula. The British adopted a "hearts and minds" strategy in 1950 in an attempt to alienate the MNLA from its civilian support. The British cut the insurrectionists off from their supply network by relocating and sequestering villages suspected of collaborating with the MNLA. The British also used secret police to infiltrate and sabotage MNLA forces from within. The most effective British tactic, however, was its offer of independence to Malaya in exchange for its help in defeating the communists.[2]

Ambassador Makins recognized the dilemma faced by the Eisenhower Administration in trying to wage war against communism in Asia and the Middle East while so many Americans saw Europe as the priority. Gallup Poll results in January 1953 showed that only fifteen percent of the Americans considered it important for the United States to block the growth of communism in Asia.[3] President Eisenhower used his inaugural address as an opportunity to illustrate the threat of global communism. He referred to a "common dignity" among "the French soldier who dies in Indo-China, the British soldier killed in Malaya," and "the American life given in Korea."[4] The president's message to Congress in February also placed the communist menace in a global context, "The freedom we cherish and defend in Europe . . . is no different from the freedom that is imperiled in Asia." He asserted that "the war in Korea" was "part of the same calculated assault . . . in Indochina and Malaya."[5] Makins believed Eisenhower's comments represented a shift from a European to "global approach to foreign policy." The ambassador detected a similar tone in Dulles' first address as secretary of state, where he blamed "the Communists" for "difficulties with nationalists in the Middle East and in Africa."[6]

February brought the Eisenhower Administration its first concerns over communist involvement in nationalist movements around the world, when

British Secretary of State for Foreign Affairs Anthony Eden announced the Anglo-Egyptian agreement recognizing the independence of Sudan. The treaty ended two years of British opposition to Egypt's claim over Sudan and marked a major step in the withdrawal of the British Empire from the Middle East and Africa. Eden described Great Britain's plan for the "Sudanisation" of the country's government and armed forces by 1956. The announcement was met with questions regarding Sudan's fitness for self-rule with a "less than 1 per cent" literacy rate and the extent to which Great Britain might be able to maintain some dominion over the country. Secretary Eden refuted the literacy statistic and noted that Sudan would have the option to join the British Commonwealth after it gained full independence.[7] Ambassador Makins detected an air of relief over the Sudan agreement in the United States, as President Eisenhower interpreted it as a sign that Egyptian Prime Minister/ President Mohamed Neguib had "decided to throw in his lot with the West" rather than the communists. Prime Minster Churchill was more suspicious, however, he viewed Neguib's Egypt as a potential threat to Great Britain's influence over the Suez Canal and Israel's nascent sovereignty.[8]

French Foreign Minister Georges Bidault visited the United States in late March to discuss Indochina. Makins reported a shift in the United States's perspective on the conflict after the meeting. He claimed the United States no longer viewed the situation as a struggle to preserve French imperialism, but now considered it a war against global communism. The ambassador attributed this change to "the context of the war in Korea" and America's "new commitment" to resist communism around the world. His report included his own interpretation of this new US policy in Asia, "if the Chinese Government took advantage of any Korean armistice to pursue an aggressive war elsewhere in the Far East, this would conflict directly with the understanding on which any armistice in Korea would rest."[9]

President Eisenhower's "Chance for Peace" speech in April spoke to his administration's duty to stop the spread of global communism, but couched this message in the rhetoric of defending freedom and self-determination around the world. He guaranteed all nations the "right to a form of government and an economic system of its own choosing" and denounced "any nation's attempt to dictate to other nations their form of government." The president claimed that peace and democracy in Korea would lead to "an end to the direct and indirect attacks upon the security of Indochina and Malaya."[10] Both statements implied that communism was the source of global instability. *Pravda* refuted Eisenhower's accusation several days later. The Russian newspaper claimed that the president's belief that Soviet communism was behind "the liberation movements among colonial and semi-colonial peoples of Asia . . . reveals ignorance of the true nature of these movements."[11] Ambassador Makins interpreted Eisenhower's speech as further evidence that the United States was taking a "strong position" against communism "on all fronts, West and East." He speculated that the United States would be "reducing aid for Europe" in "preference" for Indochina and the Middle East.[12]

Forty thousand soldiers of Ho Chi Minh's Democratic Republic of Vietnam expanded the conflict in Indochina by invading French Laos in April. Makins asserted that the "Communist attack on Laos" caused many Americans to finally recognize the "correlation of the Korean, Indo-China and Malayan fronts." Some "influential Congressmen" even suggested including a clause ending "the Communist threats against Indo-China and Malaya" in the Korean armistice. Makins observed how "concern has now replaced the apathy," as the American press, government, and public have "finally awakened to the implications in the invasion of Laos."[13] The ambassador reported that American news "commentators are content to describe Ho Chi Minh as a Soviet puppet" and Secretary Dulles announced "more military supplies are being rushed to Indo-China."[14]

American fervor over the invasion of Laos prompted Prime Minister Churchill and former Prime Minister Attlee to weigh in cautiously on communism's role in the Indochinese conflict. Churchill told the House of Commons, "we have watched with much anxiety the deterioration of the position in Indo-China," but "the sudden advance of elements of the Viet-minh forces . . . ought not lead us to conclude that it is a Soviet-inspired move," as "it might well have arisen from local circumstances and impulses."[15] Attlee warned, "one should not assume that all the troubles of the world are due to Communist initiative," as "there are other movements in the world." Attlee called "the Viet Minh attack in Laos" a "nationalist movement" and "revolt against French colonialism." He chastised the United States for drawing a hasty conclusion, "It really is an overall simplifying of the problem to put it all down to Soviet intrigue." Attlee indicted French motives as well, "colonialism belongs to a past age."[16] In a private conversation with Field Marshall Bernard Montgomery, Prime Minister Churchill claimed, "We gave up India. Why shouldn't France give up Indo-China?"[17] Makins recognized similar sentiments regarding French imperialism within the US government, as several American politicians blamed the Indochinese crisis on "France's outmoded colonial policy" and the country's insistence upon treating the conflict as a matter of empire, rather than "an international situation."[18] The ambassador noted a general American "feeling about colonialism" as "something that was quite contrary to American ideas, and couldn't be supported . . . it colored a good deal of American policy and thinking."[19]

Churchill and Attlee's speeches in the House of Commons also addressed Anglo-Egyptian relations. Churchill called Neguib a "dictator" and accused him of stonewalling Great Britain's attempts to negotiate the reduction of its military forces from the Suez Canal Zone. The prime minister asserted that the British "do not wish to keep indefinitely 80,000 men" stationed in the region and were happy to open these talks with the Egyptians, but Neguib's government "washed their hands of" the conversation by insisting upon a complete and permanent withdraw of British forces. Churchill warned that if Prime Minister Neguib's "threatening speeches" regarding the British presence in Egypt "were to be translated into action . . . we should have no choice . . . but to defend ourselves." He assured the members of the House that his stance on Egypt "is not an Imperial or Colonial enterprise," but an effort in "safeguarding the interests of the free nations in the Middle East, and also of preserving the international waterway of the Suez Canal."[20] Attlee's speech was more empathetic, "we have to realize that we are face to face with an insurgent nationalism . . . They are out for a new Egypt. We should therefore view them with a great deal of sympathy . . . they regard anything like stationing troops in their country as a violation of their sovereignty."[21] Ambassador Makins provided London with the American perspective on the Anglo-Egyptian situation. He claimed that Prime Minister Naguib "has favorable press" in the United States and most Americans feel "that the United Kingdom can ill afford to break with him." Makins reminded London that "The matter is complicated by the recurring conflict between this country's traditional anticolonialism and its appreciation of current strategic requirements" to block the spread of communism in the Middle East and North Africa.[22] Churchill remained tepid about US support for Naguib and equated it with Great Britain's recognition of Communist China.[23]

Churchill's address to the House of Commons touched upon some other British concerns in Middle East. The prime minister expressed hope that Turkey's inclusion in NATO in 1952 would lead other Middle Eastern countries to a "closer association with the Western allies." He described Great Britain as a "faithful supporter of Israel's Zionist cause" and hoped "that the Arab States will come to peace with Israel."[24] Ambassador Makins outlined Secretary Dulles' "Report on the Near East" in June and detected a pro-Arab tone running counter to Churchill's proclamations from the previous month. Makins called Dulles' report "a clear bid for better Arab-American relations" at "the risk of provoking an unfavorable reaction in Israel."[25]

Dulles made his report after visiting twelve "Near East" countries over a three-week period. The secretary exclaimed, "It is high time that the United States Government paid more attention to the Near East . . . 60 percent of the proven oil reserves of the world are in the Near East." He alluded to a "special relationship" between the United States and Saudi Arabia, "In Saudi Arabia Americans and Arabs are working together in good fellowship in the vast oil fields." In respect to the Anglo-Egyptian dispute over the "Suez Base," Dulles recounted his meeting with Prime Minister Naguib, "I am convinced that there is nothing irreconcilable between this international concern and Egyptian sovereignty . . . the base serves all Near Eastern and indeed Western security."[26] Needless to say, Churchill was troubled by the United States's lack of enthusiasm for defending British control over the Suez Canal.[27]

Concerning the Arab/Israeli Crisis, Dulles claimed that the United States sought "a step-by-step reduction of tension" to "win not only the respect and regard of the Israeli but also of the Arab peoples." He pledged the United States's commitment to the Tripartite Declaration of 1950.[28] According to the Tripartite Declaration, the United States, Great Britain, and France agreed to safeguard "the peace and stability of the Arab states and of Israel" by refusing to supply weapons to any Middle Eastern country planning to "undertake any act of aggression against any other state" or "violate frontiers" established between Israel, Egypt, Lebanon, Jordan, and Syria after the 1948 Arab/Israeli War.[29] Dulles recommended that "Israel should become part of the Near East community and cease to look upon itself . . . as alien to this community." He closed his report by placing the Middle East's effort to liberate itself from European imperialism in the context of the United States's fight against global communism, "peoples of the Near East . . . are deeply concerned about political independence . . . the Kremlin uses extreme nationalism to bait the trap by which it seeks to capture the dependent peoples." He envisioned the establishment of a Middle Eastern "collective security system" against communism.[30] The Truman Administration had already laid the foundation for this regional alliance when it established the Middle East Defense Organization with Britain, Egypt, France, and Turkey in 1951.[31]

The Middle East drew international attention in July when a British pilot disappeared in the Egyptian town of Ismailia. The British Army placed the town under martial law after the Egyptian government ignored British demands for the pilot's return. Ambassador Makins observed an impartial attitude toward the standoff in the United States, "The disappearance . . . was quite fully . . . reported," but "There has been a tendency to accuse both sides of being hot-headed."[32] The US Central Intelligence Agency's (CIA) comments on the situation reflected this nondiscriminatory position, "the British appear to be prepared to risk the consequences," but military "action will not bring closer the resumption of the suspended Anglo-Egyptian talks" pertaining to the Suez Canal. The CIA surmised it was "unlikely" that Prime Minister Naguib "wishes to engage in widespread guerilla activities" against the British, but "will use this incident as added evidence that the mere presence of British troops is a threat to Egyptian independence."[33] The apparent crisis evaporated when the British pilot turned up alive and well in England a month later.

Soviet Premier Georgy Malenkov only briefly mentioned Asia, Africa, and the Middle East in his foreign policy speech to the Supreme Soviet in August. This ambiguity led to speculation about Soviet intentions outside Europe. Ambassador Makins reported, "there is some difference of opinion on the meaning of Malenkov's statements on foreign policy, it is generally recognized that his intention is to promote neutralism in . . . Asia and the Middle East with the object of breaking up the Western alliance and isolating the United States."[34] The CIA believed Malenkov was projecting a friendly noninterventionist posture in Asia and the Middle East to paint the United States as the interloper, "Very significant is the part of Malenkov's speech devoted to the intention of the USSR to maintain good relations with Turkey, . . . Israel, . . . and Egypt" by not articulating any specific goals in those regions.[35]

President Eisenhower commented on foreign affairs at the Governor's Conference in Seattle, Washington, in August. The president illustrated why the United States needed to give more attention to the situation in Indochina, "You have seen the war in Indochina described as an outgrowth of French colonialism" and "You don't know, really, why we are so concerned with the far-off southeast corner of Asia." Eisenhower went on to explain the "domino effect" that would occur in Asia if Indochina should "become dominated by the Kremlin," as it would only be a matter of time until communism threatened India, Pakistan, Malaya, Burma, Iran, and Indonesia. He asserted that the spread of communism across Asia "would be of the most terrible significance for the United States of America-our security, our power and ability to get certain things we need from the riches of the . . . territory." The president declared, "So you see, somewhere along the line, this must be blocked. That is what the French are doing."[36] Ambassador Makins told London that "the President's remarks about the necessity of preserving Indo-China for the free world . . . marks an important development in United States foreign policy," as it represented a shift of focus from Europe to "the mainland of Asia."[37]

Both the Middle East and North Africa became the focus of international attention in August. A US/British-sponsored military *coup*, called Operation Ajax, led to the arrest of Iranian Prime Minister Mohammad Mossadeq and replaced him with General Fazlollah Zahedi. Mossadeq had fallen out of favor with the United States and Great Britain when he nationalized the Anglo-Iranian Oil Company in 1952. Ambassador Makins described the significance of the Iranian *coup* from the American perspective, "Zahedi's success and Mossadeq's surrender have raised people's hopes that at least for the present Persia will not fall under Soviet domination." He anticipated that "the United States will have to bolster the Zahedi Government with financial aid."[38] This prediction came to fruition when the US government provided Iran with forty-five million dollars of "emergency financial aid" the following month.

Prime Minister Zahedi restored the Anglo-Iranian Oil Company (later British Petroleum) in 1954 as part of an international oil consortium sharing one half of its overall profits with the Iranian government. In Morocco, the French forced Sultan Mohammed V into exile for being a secret supporter of *Istiqlal*, the Moroccan independence movement. Makins observed an unfavorable view toward this incident among most Americans, "The deposition of Sultan Sidi Mohammed Ben Youssef is regarded as a victory for reactionary forces in Morocco" and an "example of the reluctance of France to adapt her policy in dependent territories." There were additional concerns "that increased instability in Morocco may jeopardize the United States air bases there."[39]

Secretary Dulles's speech at the St. Louis American Legion in September explained United States policy in Asia as part of the larger struggle against global communism. He described "A single Chinese Communist aggressive front . . . from Korea on the north to Indochina in the south" and accused China of "training, equipping, and supplying the Communist forces in Indochina." The secretary speculated that China "might send its own army into Indochina," as it had done in Korea. He claimed that United States "material and money" support for the French in Indochina was necessary to protect American "vital interests" and "welfare" in the region.[40] Ambassador Makins surmised that Dulles used the speech as an opportunity "to praise . . . the French in Indo-China" and prime the American public for "increased United States aid" to France's war in Southeast Asia.[41]

British Consul to the United States, Alastair Maitland, suggested that "Mr. Dulles' remarks about . . . the effort and sacrifice of the French in Indo-China may have less than their desired effect on public opinion" in the United States. Maitland alluded to a "recent attack in the widely-read *Life* magazine on French policy . . . in Indo-China."[42] An editorial in the August 3 edition of *Life* described Americans as "disheartened with French conduct" in Indochina, referred to the war as "a drain on the French economy, and warned that "Ho Chi Minh's Reds are building up."[43] That same edition of *Life* also featured a full article on the war in Indochina by David Douglas Duncan, who had recently spent eight weeks in Southeast Asia. Duncan lamented, "Indochina is all but lost to the non-Communist world" due to "ineffective French tactics." He accused the French Army of keeping "hours that would delight a banker" and taking "long *siestas*." Duncan blamed French imperialism for turning Vietnamese cities into havens for opium, gambling, and corruption where "everything is for sale." He empathized with the Vietminh, referring to them as freedom fighters "led by Communists and supplied from Red China but inspired by deep nationalist feelings."[44]

Secretary Dulles explained US policy in Indochina to a multinational audience in the UN on September 17. He exclaimed, "It is no longer possible to

An oil refinery in the desert of Southern Iran. The United States and Great Britain sponsored the overthrow of Iranian Prime Minister Mossadeq after he nationalized the Anglo-Iranian Oil Company in 1952. The new prime minister, Fazlollah Zahedi, restored the company in 1954. The Anglo-Iranian Oil Company later became British Petroleum (BP). *Credit*: AL-Travelpicture.

A monument to the nearly thirty-five thousand French soldiers killed in Indochina from 1946–54 stands in Frejus, France. *Credit*: Jwackenhut.

support . . . the pretext . . . that the Communist war was designed to promote independence . . . Communist forces are seeking to gain political power by military violence . . . from a steady flow of military supplies from Communist China and Soviet Russia."[45] Ambassador Makins believed the UN responded "enthusiastically" to Dulles' speech.[46]

The United States's attention turned away from Indochina in October. First, the British government suspended the constitution of Guiana and placed the South American colony under military occupation after the nationalist People's Progressive Party won the majority of seats in the Guianan government. Prime Minster Churchill suspected that "Communist intrigues menace the normal freedom of the community" and anticipated "a bloody row Guiana."[47] Ambassador Makins assured London the Eisenhower Administration concurred with Churchill that "the People's Progressive Party is . . . a Communist rather than . . . nationalist organization" and "the unrest is the result of Communist intrigue." The United States believed that "a Communist *coup* would make British Guiana a focal point for Communist activities in the Western Hemisphere" and pose a "threat to the neighboring South American and Caribbean countries."[48] Later in the month, Israeli soldiers killed nearly seventy Arab civilians along the West Bank of the Jordan River. Makins noted that even the "frequently pro-Zionist sympathies of the American press" made "little attempt to justify the Israeli action" and many politicians "are clearly irritated by Israel's increasingly truculent conduct." In response to the atrocity, the United States government elected to "suspend American economic aid to Israel" until the Israeli government ceased all construction projects and military activity along the Jordan River. By the end of October, the Eisenhower Administration "decided to resume economic aid to Israel" after "the Israeli delegate to the United Nations assured the Security Council that Israel would suspend work on its Jordan River project."[49]

The war in Indochina was a major topic of discussion during the Bermuda Conference in December. French Foreign Minister Georges Bidault initiated the conversation, "the French Government felt that the admission of China to the United Nations should not be something to be accomplished before peace had been restored" to Indochina. He explained how "Viet Minh forces" received "increasing Chinese support in transportation" and "anti-aircraft equipment." Bidault likened the situation in Indochina to that of Korea and feared "the French might find themselves at any moment facing aggression in the air or an avalanche of land forces" from China. He pointed out that "the Chinese frontier lay close at hand" to where French and Vietminh forces were fighting. The minister also outlined recent improvements in French military strategy in Indochina. He praised General Henri Navarre for "not trying to defend everything everywhere and by choosing what to defend and what to attack." Bidault referred to the state of military affairs in Indochina as "a considerable improvement over the situation prevailing a year ago." Nevertheless, he identified some of the persistent challenges faced by French forces in Indochina, such as the "mosquitos, fever, amoebic dysentery and weakening effect of a hot climate." Bidault noted how "it is most difficult to distinguish between the peasant in his rice paddy and the enemy."[50] These French problems foreshadowed those faced by US forces in Vietnam a decade later.

Minister Bidault closed his monologue by "removing any ambiguity concerning the independence" of Indochina. He cited "the declaration of July 3 that indicated, with total independence, all powers in the hands of the French would be transferred to the Vietnamese, Cambodians and Laotians" and asserted that any notion of the war being an act of French imperialism was "a lie repeated by our Communist adversaries." Prime Minister Churchill responded with praise, support, and a touch of imperialist nostalgia, "heartfelt compliments to France for her valiant effort to preserve her empire and the cause of freedom in Indo-China . . . what a great misfortune it was when Great Britain cast away her duties in India." President Eisenhower offered the French "another aircraft carrier . . . 25 aircraft" and "some helicopters."[51]

Ambassador Makins' 1954 article in *Foreign Affairs* described colonial and post-colonial "underdeveloped countries" as the contested ground of the Cold War. The global ideological conflict forced these nations to choose to raise "their own standard of life" by adopting either a "Western or Communist" path. Makins commended Great Britain for steering its colonial and post-colonial nations away from communism. He asserted that Great Britain's "economic exploitation of colonial territories . . . is all in the past" and now the country was committed to "the development of self-government in the British colonies" and guarding "against Communist imperialism." The ambassador's article cited Great Britain's recent successes in Malaya and Guiana. Malayan support for the British fight against communism resulted in its independence in 1957. The British maintained military and political control over Guiana until the Peoples Progressive Party finally collapsed in 1957.[52]

NOTES

1. Christopher E. Goscha, "First Indochina War (1945–1954)," in *Twentieth-Century War and Conflict: A Concise Encyclopedia*, edited by Gordon Martel (West Sussex, UK: John Wiley and Sons, Ltd., 2015), 75–78.

2. Brian P. Farrell, "Malayan Emergency (1948–1960)," in *Twentieth-Century War and Conflict: A Concise Encyclopedia*, edited by Gordon Martel (West Sussex, UK: John Wiley and Sons, Ltd., 2015), 126–28.

3. Makins, "Weekly Political Summary, 3–9 January 1953."

4. Eisenhower, "Inaugural Address, 20 January 1953."

5. Eisenhower, "Annual Message to the Congress on the State of the Union, 2 February 1953."

6. Makins, "Weekly Political Summary, 17–23 January 1953;" Makins, "Weekly Political Summary, 24–30 January 1953."

7. House of Commons, "Sudan (Anglo-Egyptian Agreement), 12 February 1953," http://hansard.millbanksystems.com/commons/1953/feb/12/sudan-anglo -egyptian-agreement.

8. Makins, "Weekly Political Summary, 7–13 February 1953;" Colville, 663.

9. Makins, "Weekly Political Summary, 21–27 March 1953;" Makins, "Weekly Political Summary, 28 March-3 April 1953."

10. Eisenhower, "Chance for Peace Address, 16 April 1953."

11. Central Intelligence Agency, "Summary of *Pravda's* Reply to President Eisenhower's Address of 16 April."

12. Makins, "Weekly Political Summary, 11–17 April 1953."

13. Makins, "Weekly Political Summary, 18–24 April 1953."

14. Makins, "Weekly Political Summary, 2–8 May 1953."

15. Churchill, "Foreign Affairs, House of Commons, 11 May 1953."

16. Attlee, "Foreign Affairs, House of Commons, 12 May 1953."

17. Moran, 450.

18. Makins, "Weekly Political Summary, 2–8 May 1953."

19. Kelly, 160; Wilson, "Interview."

20. Churchill, "Foreign Affairs, House of Commons, 11 May 1953."

21. Attlee, "Foreign Affairs, House of Commons, 12 May 1953."

22. Makins, "Weekly Political Summary, 9–15 May 1953."

23. Colville, 688.

24. Churchill, "Foreign Affairs, House of Commons, 11 May 1953."

25. Makins, "Weekly Political Summary, 6–12 June 1953."

26. John F. Dulles, "Report on the Near East, 1 June 1953," https://archive.org /details/ldpd_10987272_000.

27. Moran, 461; David Boler, "Bermuda: Model for Summits to Come," in *Finest Hour: Journal of the Churchill Center*, (Spring 2003), 15.

28. Dulles, "Report on the Near East, 1 June 1953."

29. "Tripartite Declaration, 25 May 1950," http://www.jewishvirtuallibrary.org /tripartite-declaration-may-1950.

30. Dulles, "Report on the Near East, 1 June 1953."

31. Kevin Ruane, "Anglo-American Relations: The Cold War and Middle East Defense, 1953–1955," *Journal of Transatlantic Studies* (4:1 2006): 5.

32. Makins, "Weekly Political Summary, 11–17 July 1953."

33. Central Intelligence Agency. "Comment on Egyptian Situation," 13 July 1953, https://www.cia.gov/library/readingroom/docs/CIA-RDP91T01172R0002003 20012-3.pdf.

34. Makins, "Weekly Political Summary, 8–14 August 1953."

35. Central Intelligence Agency. "Reaction to Malenkov's Speech of 8 August 1953," August 14, 1953, https://www.cia.gov/library/readingroom/docs/CIA-RDP82 -00046R000200050004-0.pdf.

36. Dwight D. Eisenhower, "Remarks at the Governors' Conference, Seattle, Washington, 4 August 1953." http://www.presidency.ucsb.edu/ws/?pid=9663.

37. Makins, "Weekly Political Summary, 8–14 August 1953."

38. Makins, "Weekly Political Summary, 15–21 August 1953."

39. Makins, "Weekly Political Summary, 5–11 September 1953."

40. Dulles, "Korean Problems, 2 September 1953."

41. Makins, "Weekly Political Summary, 5–11 September 1953."

42. ibid.

43. Editorial, "Indochina, France, and the US," *Life* (August 3, 1953): 28.

44. David Douglas Duncan, "The Year of the Snake: A Time of Fear and Worry comes over Warring Indochina," *Life* (August 3, 1953): 73–79.

45. Dulles, "Address to the United Nations, 17 September 1953."

46. Makins, "Weekly Political Summary, 12–18 September 1953."

47. "Churchill's Masterly Review." *The Advertiser*, October 12, 1953. https://trove .nla.gov.au/newspaper/article/48935940; Moran, 506.

48. Makins, "Weekly Political Summary, 3–9 October 1953."

49. Makins, "Weekly Political Summary, 24–30 October 1953."

50. "United States Delegation Minutes, Bermuda, Undated," in *Foreign Relations of the United States, 1952–1954, Western European Security, Volume V, Part 2.*

51. ibid.

52. Makins, "The World Since the War: The Third Phase," 10–12; Farrell, "Malayan Emergency (1948–1960)," 129.

Chapter Four

US Cold War Policy in 1953

Between Deterrence and Détente

US foreign policy was in an overall state of transition in 1953. The coalition that had won the Second World War dissolved and the new challenges of the Cold War emerged. The postwar international landscape presented the United States with a mixture of old and new policymaking options. On one hand, the United States pursued the traditional balance-of-power through deterrence approach to global affairs by forging alliances and maintaining a large military with the latest technology. The United States formed NATO with Great Britain, France, Italy, Belgium, Canada, Denmark, Luxembourg, the Netherlands, Norway, and Iceland in 1949. NATO was a classic military alliance where "an armed attack against one or more" of its members "shall be considered an attack against them all." The threat of the "use of armed force" in retaliation for such an attack served as the deterrent against aggression.[1] US foreign policy in 1953 also included the deterrent of its atomic weapons arsenal. The United States developed the hydrogen bomb in 1952, an atomic device more powerful than those used in 1945. At the same time, the United States explored the possibilities of collective security and international dialogue by taking a leadership role in the UN. The UN provided its members with a forum for peaceful diplomacy, "economic collaboration," and "mutual aid." In addition to these policy options, Prime Minister Churchill spent much of 1953 working to convince the President Eisenhower to engage in direct dialogue with Soviet leadership.

President Truman's January farewell address reflected on his administration's work to establish a more eclectic set of foreign policy options for the United States. Truman credited his time in office with "carving out a new set of policies to attain peace" by forming an alliance of the "free world" in NATO and adopting a "world leadership" role in the UN. The outgoing president echoed his 1947 "containment" address to Congress by describing the

Cold War as an "all-embracing . . . conflict between those who love freedom and those who would lead the world back into slavery." He warned, "If we let the Republic of Korea go under, some other country would be next, and then another." Truman utilized the same "domino effect" metaphor when he urged Congress to support Greece in its fight against communism in 1947. President Truman's farewell speech also alluded to nuclear deterrence, "Starting an atomic war is totally unthinkable for rational men."[2] Ambassador Makins referred to this portion of the address as Truman's last "warning to Stalin."[3]

President Eisenhower's inaugural address took up the mantel of his predecessor proclaiming, "destiny has laid upon our country the responsibility of the free world's leadership." He pledged to "maintain American military strength" and support "deserving allies" against global communism. The new president also promised to work "within the framework of the United Nations" and "never use our strength to try to impress upon another people our own cherished political and economic institutions."[4]

Ambassador Makins recognized the possibility for US policy changes under the Eisenhower Administration. In January, he reported on Secretary Dulles' recent remarks about the "liberation" of nations "threatened" by Soviet "encirclement."[5] Dulles declared that working to simply "contain" global communism was no longer sufficient. Instead, he advocated for "the liberation of" those living under communist domination.[6] Makins viewed Dulles' proposed course of action as an expansion of President Truman's "containment" strategy, rooted in "the idea that democracy can be spread by the methods used so successfully to sell soap."[7]

In February, President Eisenhower told Congress that "the United States rejects . . . any international agreement . . . perverted to bring about the subjugation of free peoples." He claimed that the 1945 Yalta agreement had "been twisted . . . to help the enslavement of peoples."[8] Ambassador Makins explained to London how these remarks were aimed at "Soviet despotism" and its "persecution of minorities in Iron Curtain countries," but "cast no aspersions" upon presidents Franklin Roosevelt and Truman's wartime arrangements with Premier Stalin.[9] When asked about "World War II agreements" and the "criticism of your two predecessors having made those agreements," Eisenhower made it clear that he had "no interest in going back and raking up the ashes of the dead past."[10]

President Eisenhower's message to Congress described "mutual cooperation" and "mutual security" within the UN as a major part of US strategy against "Communist aggression." He also asserted that a "powerful deterrent is defensive power" and "No enemy is likely to attempt an attack foredoomed to failure." Eisenhower further qualified his call for military deterrence, "Because we have incontrovertible evidence that Soviet Russia possesses atomic

Remnants of the Iron Curtain in the present Czech Republic (former communist Czechoslovakia). Barricades like this one divided communist countries in Central and Eastern Europe from the rest of the continent during the Cold War. Winston Churchill used the term "Iron Curtain" to refer to these communist countries in a speech in 1946. *Credit:* andriano_cz.

weapons, this kind of protection becomes sheer necessity."[11] When asked if he would be "willing to go out of this country to meet with Stalin," Eisenhower responded, "I would meet anybody, anywhere, where I thought there was the slightest chance of doing any good."[12] Ambassador Makins cautioned London not to be too optimistic about a US/Soviet summit, "Since these remarks were made in reply to a journalist's questions, they are not construed . . . as being a hint that President Eisenhower has any plans for meeting with Stalin."[13]

The possibility for major changes in the international landscape emerged with the death of Premier Stalin in March. Prime Minister Churchill was especially hopeful "that Stalin's death may lead to a relaxation in tension."[14] Despite the good news, Ambassador Makins noticed an air of apprehension in the United States, "it is not generally believed that a lowering of the temperature of the cold war can be expected" with Stalin's passing. Makins observed an anxious uncertainty concerning Stalin's successor, Georgy Malenkov, "the succession of Malenkov . . . may well be more dangerous to world peace than Stalin's dictatorship." British Foreign Secretary Anthony Eden and Chancellor of the Exchequer R. A. Butler were visiting with President Eisenhower and Secretary Dulles when the Soviet Premier passed away. Makins called Eden and Butler's "ministerial visit . . . a major success . . . toward the collective approach." He believed the new climate of change would strengthen Anglo-American relations and bolster "British and Commonwealth leadership" in the Cold War world.[15]

An attack by Soviet fighter jets on a NATO bomber over Germany threatened the prospects for improved US/Soviet relations just a few days after Stalin's passing. Seven British airmen died when the bomber went down. Nevertheless, Ambassador Makins was impressed by the level of "calm and restraint" in the US's reaction to the incident, "There is little disposition to believe that the Kremlin wants to precipitate a crisis." According to the Ambassador, most Americans were content to blame the attack on "over-zealous frontier defense" and "trigger-happy pilots." He did note, however, that the hostile act decreased the "inclination to believe that Stalin's death will make any immediate difference to the cold war."[16]

In a speech to the Supreme Soviet in March, Premier Malenkov stated that "troublesome and unresolved questions may be resolved by peaceful negotiations" with the United States. Ambassador Makins noted that some American newspapers reported on Malenkov's statement as a "peace feeler."[17] On the other hand, much of the American public remained "wary of booby traps and Trojan horses" hidden behind the new "Soviet peace offensive." Makins also detected "some annoyance" within the US State Department over Malenkov's speech. State Department officials claimed that the new Soviet Premier was simply echoing the same empty rhetoric "put up for years" since the Second World War.[18]

President Eisenhower's "Chance for Peace" address in April represented his most comprehensive overview of US foreign policy since his inauguration and served as an unofficial response to Malenkov's "peace feeler." He presented "a few clear precepts, which govern" American "conduct in world affairs." The president spoke of peace through the collective security of the UN, "No nation's security and well-being can be lastingly achieved in isolation but only in effective cooperation with fellow nations." He advocated for collective security over nuclear deterrence, "A nation's hope of lasting peace cannot be firmly based upon any race in armaments but rather upon just relations and honest understanding with all other nations." Eisenhower asserted that military buildup and weapons of mass destruction only cause "perpetual fear and tension . . . under the cloud of threatening war." He suggested that the UN be responsible for regulating "the sizes of the military and security forces of all nations" and the "prohibition of atomic weapons." Eisenhower's speech noted the change of leadership in the Soviet Union and hinted at the possibility for summit, "an era ended with the death of Joseph Stalin . . . It is a moment that calls upon the governments of the world to speak their intentions with simplicity and honesty . . . the new Soviet leadership now has a precious opportunity to awaken . . . and help turn the tide of history." He closed his address by placing the initiative with Premier Malenkov, "What is the Soviet Union ready to do?"[19]

Ambassador Makins believed Eisenhower's UN "disarmament proposal" was "beyond the realms of practical politics." The Ambassador interpreted the "Chance for Peace" address to mean that a US/Soviet summit was on hold "Until the Kremlin gives further signs of genuinely desiring a *détente*."[20] The Russian newspaper *Pravda* responded to the "Chance for Peace" speech by blaming the United States for all the post-WWII problems Eisenhower alluded to in his address. *Pravda* attributed the nuclear arms race to the United States's aggressive policies and pursuit of global domination and asserted that it was the United States's responsibility to take the next step toward initiating a summit.[21]

Prime Minister Churchill began his own push for a US/Soviet summit in May. His address on foreign affairs in the House of Common described a "change of attitude . . . in the Kremlin since the death of Stalin." Churchill announced that it was now "the policy of Her Majesty's Government to . . . welcome every sign of improvement in our relations with Russia." The prime minster expressed empathy with the Soviet security concerns, "I do not believe that the immense problem of reconciling the security of Russia with the freedom and safety of Western Europe is insoluble . . . Russia has a right to feel assured that . . . the terrible events of the Hitler invasion will never be repeated." Churchill closed his speech with a call for "a conference on the highest level," without a "rigid agenda," and the simple goal of fostering a "feeling among those gathered together that they might do something better than tear the human race, including themselves, into bits."[22] Former Prime Minster Clement Attlee supported the current Prime Minister's call for summit, "we all welcome the signs of a change in the attitude on the part of Soviet Russia." Attlee believed "a conference on the highest level" would lead to "piecemeal solutions of individual problems" and a "greater understanding, by us of them and them of us."[23] Churchill had advocated for summit earlier in the Cold War. He criticized "the old doctrine of a balance of power" and suggested "a good understanding on all points with Russia" in his famous "Iron Curtain" speech of 1946.[24]

Ambassador Makins informed London of the American reactions to Churchill's plea for summit. He noted a "deep-rooted distrust of Yalta-like agreements" and a belief that "the Soviet Union's good faith must first be demonstrated" or proven before a meeting could occur. Some American politicians harbored a "resentment that the Prime Minister has stolen the initiative" from the United States and believed Churchill's proposal "undermines the firm stand taken by the United States."[25]

Ambassador Makins reported more promising news in late May, "recent opinion polls have shown that the public overwhelmingly approves a Big Four meeting." Furthermore, the Eisenhower Administration proposed a high-level meeting between the United States, Great Britain, and France in Bermuda. Makins noticed a deliberate "reticence about the topics to be discussed at Bermuda" and saw "no encouragement" to indicate "whether the meeting will prove to be a preliminary to a Big Four conference with the Soviet Union."[26] When asked if "the forthcoming Bermuda conference" would "lead to a Big Four conference, with Russia included," the President Eisenhower stated that he did not think "it is necessarily going to lead to such a meeting."[27] Consul Maitland remained optimistic nonetheless, "This decision . . . will mean that the seed sown by the Prime Minister will take longer to germinate."[28]

American efforts to establishing alliances against global communism dominated the next several months of US foreign affairs. The Eisenhower Administration pressed hard for the formation of a European Defense Community (EDC). The 1947 Marshall Plan included a vague endorsement for a unified Europe. The plan succeeded in creating a collaborative program for "the rehabilitation of the economic structure of Europe," but failed to evolve into a "supranational" alliance for the long-term economic and military integration of the continent.[29] Belgium, France, Italy, Luxembourg, the Netherlands, and West Germany signed a tentative EDC agreement in 1952, but the treaty still needed to be ratified by each nation's government. President

Eisenhower's inaugural address implored, "In Europe, we ask that enlightened and inspired leaders of Western nations strive with renewed vigor to make the unity of their peoples a reality."[30] Ambassador Makins speculated that the new administration would use "cutting off American aid as a stick with which to beat Western Europe into effective unity." One of his January report to London noted Eisenhower's concerns over "France's reliability as an ally" in "the furtherance of European unity and the early creation of a European Army."[31]

Foreign ministers from the six European countries met in Rome in February to discuss the ratification of the EDC. According to Ambassador Makins, this meeting ignited a "dramatic revival of . . . the unity and defense of the West."[32] President Eisenhower's message to Congress that month called for "cooperation among the nations of Europe" with "a more closely integrated economic and political system" and "military readiness."[33] Nevertheless, the Eisenhower Administration remained skeptical about French enthusiasm for the EDC. After French Foreign Minister Georges Bidault visited with the president in March, Makins detected "an undercurrent of feeling that France is not really prepared to give full support to the European Defense Community."[34] Meanwhile, United States's confidence in West Germany's dependability as an ally against the Soviet Union increased. Makins referred to West German Chancellor Konrad Adenauer's visit to the United States in April as "an unqualified success." He informed London that "The man-in-the-street feels that the Germans are dependable in a way that the French are not."[35]

Prime Minister Churchill advocated for the establishment of the EDC in his speech on foreign affairs in the House of Commons in May. He declared, "we sincerely hope before long to have, the European Defense Community." Churchill made it clear that Great Britain would not be joining the EDC, "We are not members of the European Defense Community, nor do we intend to merge in a Federal European system." The prime minister did, however, pledge to collaborate with the EDC, "On the military side, we will ensure effective and continuous cooperation . . . On the political side, we intend to consult constantly."[36] The prime minister first alluded to a European defense federation in his "Iron Curtain" speech in 1946, "The safety of the world, ladies and gentlemen, requires unity in Europe."[37]

US Senate Majority Leader Robert A. Taft called US participation in alliances into question when he demanded a return to isolationism in Congress in May. Ambassador Makins highlighted the many negative responses to Taft's proclamation, "the idea that the United States can go-it-alone is rejected most decisively on the ground that politically it would fulfil the dearest wish of the Kremlin . . . and foredoom the ideological battle against communism." The ambassador described President Eisenhower responding "with an unequivocal 'no' when asked whether he shared Taft's view."[38] In fact, US alliance aspirations were expanding. Makins reported on a recent discussion in Congress regarding "the creation of a Pacific counterpart of NATO." Secretary Dulles' June "Report on the Near East" spoke of the "possibility" of expanding the "Middle East Defense Organization."[39]

The results of the Italian general election in June cast further doubt upon the EDC. Italy's pro-EDC centrist coalition barely retained half the seats in parliament. Ambassador Makins described "considerable disappointment at the outcome of the Italian elections" and "prospects of ratification of the EDC are thought to be poor."[40] The ambassador reported on conversations in the US House of Representatives Foreign Affairs Committee about withholding "military aid for Europe . . . until the European Defense Treaty is ratified." Congress acted on this recommendation and passed a bill reducing the European defense budget by $100 million.[41]

Conversations over the possibility of a US/Soviet summit reemerged in late June when strikes and riots broke out in Soviet-controlled East Berlin and hundreds of other towns across Communist East Germany. Ambassador Makins observed how some Americans regarded the unrest in East Germany as evidence that the Iron Curtain was crumbling from within, "The disturbances in Eastern Germany are thought to demand a reassessment of Western political strategy," as many Americans believed "the tide is turning against Soviet imperialism." This caused some in the United States to think there was no longer a need for a summit with Soviets, "riots in Berlin . . . are already being used as an argument against an early four power meeting." Consul Maitland's optimism continued, however, "I don't altogether agree about the lessening prospect of US agreement to any four-power meeting. I shall be very surprised if after Bermuda the President does not accept this."[42]

Ambassador Makins notified London in July of President Eisenhower's decision to postpone the meeting in Bermuda, "recent events behind the Iron Curtain . . . have convinced . . . members of the Administration and of Congress that the proper strategy for the West is to wait and see." Makins' prediction on the "disturbances in Eastern Europe" was that "American help for captive peoples will be limited to words of encouragement." Nevertheless, "The White House announced . . . $15 million worth of surplus foodstuffs . . . to Eastern Germany" within a week after the riots. The ambassador considered this relief effort "a propaganda and political move designed to put the Kremlin on the spot."[43] As Makins anticipated, "the distribution of food parcels to residents of the Soviet Zone in Germany" was "receiving much publicity" in the American press.[44] Meanwhile, any hope for the Iron Curtain imploding from the inside had already evaporated. Soviet troops brought a violent end to the East German uprisings.

Premier Malenkov's address to the Supreme Soviet in August made firm statements in regard to maintaining a block of Soviet-friendly countries in Central and Eastern Europe and the Soviet Union's weapons of mass destruction capabilities. The US Central Intelligence Agency (CIA) analyzed the speech and determined that Malenkov believed "the West is preparing for an aggressive war against the USSR" and that the United States "should not expect the USSR to leave" Central and Eastern Europe.[45] Ambassador Makin surmised that "Malenkov's statement to the Supreme Soviet" meant that "the United States no longer had the monopoly of the hydrogen bomb." Despite the overall threatening tone of the Soviet Premier's speech, the CIA found some evidence to suggest that "Malenkov believes . . . coexistence is possible."[46] This left the door open for a possible US/Soviet summit.

Ambassador Makins notified London of the Soviet Union's first hydrogen bomb test in August, "an announcement of the Atomic Energy Commission that some such explosion took place on August 12." The ambassador believed this would rekindle the Eisenhower Administration's "demand for some form of limitation of atomic weapons" in the UN.[47] Secretary Dulles addressed the atomic threat in a speech to the American Bar Association in Boston, Massachusetts. He called for a "voluntary association of free nations," including the "North Atlantic community," the "American republics," and "the Pacific" to stand against "the Soviet-dominated world" in the name of "collective self-defense." The secretary also suggested that the UN needed to revise its "pre-atomic-age charter" to include the "disarmament and the regulation" of weapons of mass destruction.[48]

Secretary Dulles continued to articulate his threat-management plan in his speech to the American Legion in St. Louis in September. He used the "domino effect" metaphor to illustrate how global communism, "if unchecked, would . . . imperil the United States." The secretary criticized those who "think that peace is won merely by pacifism." He called for "international cooperation" to make "unlikely . . . another act of unprovoked military aggression."[49] Ambassador Makins described Dulles's description of US foreign policy as going "further than the Administration has gone" in leaving "potential aggressors in no doubt about American intentions." The Ambassador viewed Dulles's lucid explanation of US policy as cautionary response to the "Russian possession of the H-bomb."[50]

Ambassador Makins reported on several events in September that affirmed Secretary Dulles' global "collective self-defense" initiative. Japanese Crown Prince Akihito's visit to the United States showed "how far public sentiment has changed towards the . . . ex-enemy . . . Japan is not only welcomed as a strategically important ally in Asia but is accepted as an ideological associate in the battle against Communism."[51] The meeting of the Australia, New

Zealand, and US Security Treaty (ANZUS) in Washington, DC, was further evidence of the United States's "determination to resist Communist aggression in the Pacific." The United States had entered into the ANZUS Treaty with Australian and New Zealand in 1951 to affirm "peace in the Pacific Area . . . so that no potential aggressor could be under the illusion that any of them stand alone in the Pacific Area."[52] Makins anticipated that the ANZUS council was taking steps toward "integrating the Japanese and Philippine defense pacts" into its alliance.[53]

Secretary Dulles also addressed the UN in September. Dulles assured the UN that US foreign policy "does not call for exporting revolution or inciting other to violence." He acknowledged the "15 nations that have been brought into the Soviet camp." The secretary claimed that United States "can understand the particular desire of the Russian people to have close neighbors who are friendly" and "does not want to see Russia encircled by hostile peoples." Nevertheless, Dulles reiterated the US commitment to the right of "Russia's neighbors to enjoy national independence."[54] Ambassador Makins viewed Dulles's speech as a departure from his usual promise to "liberate" countries under communist control. Instead, the speech seemed to hint at an acceptance of a balance of power between US and Soviet spheres of influence. Makins also noted "Dulles' recommendation that the United Nations proceed with the 'technical analysis' required to prepare the ground for an agreement to limit armaments." Overall, the Ambassador praised Dulles' UN address as an "effective portrayal of the value of collective security." Makins cited a recent Gallup Poll showing sixty-six percent of Americans in support the UN.[55]

Although Secretary Dulles' UN speech appeared to indicate a willingness to coexist with global communism, the United States continued to rally European nations against the Soviet Union. The United States signed a military agreement with Spain to deter "the danger that threatens the western world . . . through foresighted measures," including the American use of Spanish military bases and US funding for the improvement of Spain's armed forces.[56] Ambassador Makins observed a "mixed" reaction to the US/Spain agreement. While most Americans recognized "the importance of completing the defense perimeter in Western Europe," many harbored a "distaste for the Franco regime."[57] *Generalissimo* Francisco Franco had emerged as the fascist political leader of Spain during its civil war in the 1930s. His anti-communist ideology made him an ally of the Eisenhower Administration, but his authoritarianism, militarism, and ultra-nationalism made him unpopular with the American people.

October brought some "conflicting statements" concerning "the Soviet Union's atomic strength and the threat it presents to the United States." US Director of Defense Mobilization Arthur S. Flemming claimed that the Soviets possessed a hydrogen bomb with the capability to drop it on the United States. Secretary of Defense Charles E. Wilson believed the Soviets had the bomb, but lacked an intercontinental delivery system. Defense Administrator Val Peterson doubted that the Soviets even had a hydrogen bomb.[58] In a speech in Atlantic City, New Jersey, President Eisenhower announced that "the mysteries of the atom are known to Russia" and America's "physical security has almost totally disappeared before the long-range bomber and the destructive power of a single bomb." Eisenhower advocated for deterrence through military preparedness, "The free world must build, maintain and pay for a military might assuring us reasonable safety from attack."[59] Prime Minister Churchill voiced a slightly more hopeful perspective in a speech to the House of Commons, "the probabilities of another world war have become more remote . . . when the advance of destructive weapons enables everyone to kill everybody else, nobody will want to kill anyone at all."[60] Ambassador Makins expressed "hope . . . that the atomic arms race might be halted . . . and a catastrophic war avoided" through "an understanding with Russia." He believed the threat of nuclear annihilation had swayed the Eisenhower Administration "in favor of further negotiations with the Kremlin."[61]

Prime Minister Churchill renewed his push for a US/Soviet summit in a speech to the Conservative Party in October. He suggested that a top-level meeting between the United States and the Soviet Union would be a better alternative "than tearing and blasting each other to pieces." At the same time, Churchill reaffirmed Great Britain's commitment to military deterrence, "Britain, like the United States, will maintain her forces in Europe" and "promote the formation of a European army."[62] Ambassador Makins alleged that American discussions concerning "a top level conference with the Russians" have been "stimulated by the Prime Minister's speech." He reported "an evolutionary change . . . on East-West Relations . . . accepting things substantially as they are" and a move toward "diplomatic action" over "military containment." The Ambassador detected some concern in the United States that "the Prime Minister may insist on 'going it alone' in arranging a meeting with Malenkov."[63] This anxiety was not unfounded. Churchill did "reserve the right to" extend "a hand to grasp the paw of the Russian bear" and "see Malenkov alone" earlier in the year.[64]

Meanwhile, the Soviet Union's hydrogen bomb test was having its impact on US defense strategy and spending. Consul Maitland described "numerous" US congressmen pushing for the "withdrawal of ground forces from Europe" due to the "increased expenditure on . . . the atom bomb." Ambassador Makins reported on a US Department of Defense's proposal to "withdraw the bulk of its ground forces from Europe" to allow for "strengthening the Air Force and increasing the stockpile of atomic weapons." US Secretary of

Defense Charles Wilson claimed "that American troops overseas might well be reduced in numbers."[65] Makins believed "nuclear weapons" fit well with the American belief that "mechanical genius will ultimately take much of the human risk out of war." Nevertheless, there was some opposition to the potential shift from conventional military forces to an arsenal of weapons of mass destruction. Prominent news reporter Walter Lippman believed atomic weapons were useful in cases of total war, but "far less effective as instruments of national policy." Lippman asserted that the removal of American military forces from Europe would cause US "influence . . . to decline" around the world.[66]

Prospects for a high-level US/Soviet summit turned bleak in November with the so-called "Soviet Note" demanding "a virtual scrapping of the European Defense Community and a dismantling of the NATO base system." President Eisenhower referred to the Soviet *communique* as "negative" and filled with "impossible conditions."[67] Surprisingly, a November Gallup Poll still showed seventy-nine percent of Americans "in favor of a meeting of Eisenhower, Churchill, Laniel, and Malenkov." Ambassador Makins considered this to be a sign "that the end of one diplomatic road has been reached and that another is about to begin." He believed that the upcoming "Big Three" meeting in Bermuda would "show the Kremlin that the leading Western nations stand united and firm but ready to negotiate on any reasonable basis."[68]

When the Bermuda Conference finally commenced in December, Prime Minister Churchill intended to persuade President Eisenhower to arrange a "Big Three" talk with Premier Malenkov. Much to Prime Minister's dismay, Eisenhower made it clear that he would not meet with Malenkov until a preliminary summit took place between US and Soviet foreign ministers. Churchill reacted bitterly, "The underlings don't want a Four Power Conference at this highest level; they want a meeting of the Foreign Secretaries. Nothing will come of that." He blamed Secretary Dulles for Eisenhower's reluctance, "everything is left to Dulles . . . the President is no more than a ventriloquist's doll."[69]

When French Prime Minister Laniel joined Churchill and Eisenhower in Bermuda, the conversation shifted to nuclear proliferation and the President's upcoming UN speech. President Truman discussed the possibility of establishing some kind of international oversight of nuclear technology in 1945, just months after he authorized the use of weapons of mass destruction against Imperial Japan. Ambassador Makins participated in these 1945 conversations while working as a minister in the British Embassy in Washington, DC. The Atomic Energy Act of 1946 (McMahon Act) placed the development of all commercial and military nuclear technology in the United States under the supervision of the Atomic Energy Commission. In order to guard against the spread of nuclear weapons capabilities to other countries, the act gave both the commission and the president the authority to limit and suppress the "dissemination of related technical information" in the name of "national defense."[70] With the United States no longer the sole possessor of weapons of mass destruction in 1953, President Eisenhower sought to establish international rules and limitations concerning nuclear technology. Eisenhower informed his peers in Bermuda that he intended to use his address to convince the UN to develop a program for regulating atomic weapons worldwide.

Prime Minister Churchill made one last plea for a top-level summit before the conference adjourned. He reiterated his belief that Stalin's death represented an opportunity for "real change" and that the Soviets would be willing to loosen their grip on the "Iron Curtain" if the West would offer "reassurance that they would not have another dose of Hitler" along their western border. Needless to say, the prime minister left Bermuda dissatisfied. He accused Secretary Dulles's self-serving ambition for sabotaging his plan to arrange a "Big Three" summit and called Eisenhower too "simple minded" to appreciate the complexity of the situation, "They want the Kremlin to give up" European territory which "they themselves gave up to Stalin" during the Second World War.[71]

Ambassador Makins lamented that "the Bermuda Conference has had bad press" in the United States. The overwhelming opinion was that it "did not arrive anywhere" and "there seems little enthusiasm . . . for a repetition of the Bermuda meeting."[72] Despite Makins' negative impressions, President Eisenhower spoke positively about the Bermuda Conference in his UN speech, "from our joint Bermuda *communique*, the United States, Great Britain, and France have agreed promptly to meet with the Soviet Union . . . Let no one say that we shun the conference table." The president echoed Prime Minister Churchill's thoughts on Soviet influence over Central and Eastern Europe, "We never have, we never will, propose or suggest that the Soviet Union surrender what is rightfully theirs."[73]

The remainder of President Eisenhower's UN address focused on nuclear proliferation. He admitted that the United States's atomic arsenal "increases daily" and contains weapons "25 times as powerful" as those used in 1945. Eisenhower confirmed that "the Soviet Union has exploded a series of atomic devices" and warned that a nuclear conflict would result in destruction "so great that such an aggressor's land would be laid waste." In the face of this kind of mutual annihilation, "no sane member of the human race could discover victory in such desolation." The president pledged that the United States "is instantly prepared . . . to seek an acceptable solution to the atomic armaments race" and recommended the formation of a UN disarmament commission.[74]

Saint Georges, Bermuda was the site of the 1953 Bermuda Conference between Prime Minister Churchill, President Eisenhower, and Prime Minister Laniel. Churchill hoped the meeting would lead to a summit with Soviet Premier Malenkov, but a meeting between Soviet and US heads of state would not occur until 1955. *Credit:* mdgmorris.

Secretary Dulles reflected positively on the Bermuda Conference when he made his endorsement for the EDC at a NATO meeting in Paris. He advocated for Western "unity as a permanent condition" to counter the Soviet Union's "intention to promote our disunity by all the means at their command." The secretary cited the meeting in Bermuda as an important step toward establishing "intimate and durable cooperation between the United Kingdom and the United States forces and the forces of the European Defense Community." He warned that the failure to form the EDC would leave "grave doubt whether continental Europe could be made a place of safety."[75] Some NATO members construed Dulles's remarks as a veiled threat to withdraw US military support from Europe if the EDC failed to materialize. After all, Congress had already reduced its European defense budget earlier in the year and US Chief of the State Department's Division of Western European Affairs Douglas MacArthur II stated that further budget cuts would force the US military to withdraw to the outskirts of Europe (Iceland, Turkey, North Africa, etc.)[76] Prime Minister Churchill also alluded to "punitive measures" against Continental Europe if it did not ratify the EDC, "if American troops were withdrawn from Europe British troops would leave too" and "France may become . . . a satellite of Russia."[77]

Ambassador Makins' 1954 publication in *Foreign Affairs* recognized the Soviet Union as a continued threat to world peace, with "no reduction in the size and efficiency of" its armed forces, "the latest thermonuclear and ballistic weapons," and the "principal aim . . . to maintain Soviet control over Eastern Europe." Nevertheless, he expressed hope that the UN would foster "international cooperation" and "reduce the burden and the threat of . . . atomic weapons, by any means which ensures adequate international control." He also remained optimistic about Prime Minister Churchill's vision for a US/Soviet summit. Makins believed the United States would eventually come to realize that "negotiation" is not "synonymous with appeasement." In the meantime, the world would need to maintain "peaceful coexistence" and "a balance resting on peace through strength." The Ambassador described military deterrence and alliances as the primary components of this peaceful balance, "the free world must maintain the military strength and organization which is essential to keep the equilibrium." He contented that NATO and the "movements toward European integration" were critical to saving the world from being "swallowed by expanding Communism."[78]

NOTES

1. "North Atlantic Treaty, 4 April 1949," https://www.nato.int/cps/ie/natohq/official_texts_17120.htm.

2. Truman, "Farwell Address to the American People, 15 January 1953;" Harry S. Truman, "Address before a Joint Session of Congress, 12 March 1947," http://avalon.law.yale.edu/20th_century/trudoc.asp.

3. Makins, "Weekly Political Summary, 10–16 January 1953."

4. Eisenhower, "Inaugural Address, 20 January 1953."

5. Makins, "Weekly Political Summary, 24–30 January 1953."

6. John F. Dulles, "Statement on Liberation Policy, 15 January 1953," http://teachingamericanhistory.org/library/document/statement-on-liberation-policy/.

7. Makins, "Weekly Political Summary, 24–30 January 1953."

8. Eisenhower, "Annual Message to the Congress on the State of the Union, 2 February 1953."

9. Makins, "Weekly Political Summary, 14–20 February 1953."

10. Eisenhower, "News Conference, 17 February 1953;" Dwight D. Eisenhower, "News Conference, 25 February 1953," http://www.presidency.ucsb.edu/ws/index.php?pid=9656.

11. Eisenhower, "Annual Message to the Congress on the State of the Union, 2 February 1953."

12. Eisenhower, "News Conference, 25 February 1953."

13. Makins, "Weekly Political Summary, 21–27 February 1953."

14. Moran, 429.

15. Makins, "Weekly Political Summary, 28 February-6 March 1953."

16. Makins, "Weekly Political Summary, 7–13 March 1953."

17. Makins, "Weekly Political Summary, 14–20 March 1953."

18. Makins, "Weekly Political Summary, 28 March–3 April 1953."

19. Eisenhower, "Chance for Peace Address, 16 April 1953."

20. Makins, "Weekly Political Summary, 11–17 April 1953;" Makins, "Weekly Political Summary, 18–24 April 1953."

21. Central Intelligence Agency, "Summary of *Pravda's* Reply to President Eisenhower's Address of 16 April."

22. Churchill, "Foreign Affairs, House of Commons, 11 May 1953."

23. Attlee, "Foreign Affairs, House of Commons, 12 May 1953."

24. Winston S. Churchill, "Iron Curtain Speech, 5 March 1946," https://sourcebooks.fordham.edu/mod/churchill-iron.asp.

25. Makins, "Weekly Political Summary, 9–15 May 1953."

26. Makins, "Weekly Political Summary, 16–22 May 1953."

27. Eisenhower, "News Conference, 28 May 1953."

28. Makins, "Weekly Political Summary, 16–22 May 1953."

29. George C. Marshall, "Marshall Plan Speech, Harvard University, 5 June 1947," https://www.marshallfoundation.org/marshall/the-marshall-plan/marshall-plan-speech/; Brooks, "Interview;" Wilson, "Interview."

30. Eisenhower, "Inaugural Address, 20 January 1953."

31. Makins, "Weekly Political Summary, 17–23 January 1953;" Makins, "Weekly Political Summary, 24–30 January 1953."

32. Makins, "Weekly Political Summary, 21–27 February 1953."

33. Eisenhower, "Annual Message to the Congress on the State of the Union, 2 February 1953."

34. Makins, "Weekly Political Summary, 21–27 March 1953."

35. Makins, "Weekly Political Summary, 4–10 April 1953."

36. Churchill, "Foreign Affairs, House of Commons, 11 May 1953."

37. Churchill, "Iron Curtain Speech, 5 March 1946."

38. Makins, "Weekly Political Summary, 23–29 May 1953."

39. Makins, "Weekly Political Summary, 30 May–5 June 1953."

40. Makins, "Weekly Political Summary, 6–12 June 1953."

41. Makins, "Weekly Political Summary, 13–19 June 1953."

42. Makins, "Weekly Political Summary, 13–19 June 1953;" Makins, "Weekly Political Summary, 20–26 June 1953."

43. Makins, "Weekly Political Summary, 27 June–3 July 1953."

44. Makins, "Weekly Political Summary, 4–10 July 1953."

45. Central Intelligence Agency, "Reaction to Malenkov's Speech of 8 August 1953," 14 August 1953.

46. Makins, "Weekly Political Summary, 8–14 August 1953."

47. Makins, "Weekly Political Summary, 15–21 August 1953."

48. John F. Dulles, "US Constitution and UN Charter: An Appraisal, 26 August 1953." https://babel.hathitrust.org/cgi/pt?id=umn.31951d03563129p.

49. Dulles, "Korean Problems, 2 September 1953."

50. Makins, "Weekly Political Summary, 28 August–4 September 1953."

51. Makins, "Weekly Political Summary, 5–11 September 1953."

52. "ANZUS Treaty, 1 September 1951." http://avalon.law.yale.edu/20th_century /usmu002.asp.

53. Makins, "Weekly Political Summary, 5–11 September 1953."

54. Dulles, "Address to the United Nations, 17 September 1953."

55. Makins, "Weekly Political Summary, 12–18 September 1953."

56. "Military Facilities in Spain: Agreement between the United States and Spain, 26 September 1953." http://avalon.law.yale.edu/20th_century/sp1953.asp.

57. Makins, "Weekly Political Summary, 25 September–2 October 1953."

58. Makins, "Weekly Political Summary, 3–9 October 1953."

59. Dwight D. Eisenhower, "Address at the Sixth National Assembly of the United Church Women, Atlantic City, New Jersey, 6 October 1953." http://www.presidency .ucsb.edu/ws/index.php?pid=9718.

60. Moran, 525.

61. Makins, "Weekly Political Summary, 3–9 October 1953."

62. Trevor Smith, "Churchill's Great Comeback," *The Advertiser*, October 12, 1953. https://trove.nla.gov.au/newspaper/article/48935702.

63. Makins, "Weekly Political Summary, 10–16 October 1953;" Makins, "Weekly Political Summary, 17–23 October 1953."

64. Moran, 436; ibid., 461; Colville, 667.

65. Makins, "Weekly Political Summary, 17–23 October 1953."

66. Makins, "Weekly Political Summary, 24–30 October 1953."

67. Dwight D. Eisenhower, "News Conference, 4 November 1953." http://www.presidency.ucsb.edu/ws/index.php?pid=9754.

68. Makins, "Weekly Political Summary, 31 October–6 November 1953."

69. Colville, 679; Moran, 536–37; ibid., 540.

70. "Atomic Energy Act, 22 April 1946," http://www.nuclearfiles.org/menu/library/treaties/atomic-energy-act/trty_atomic-energy-act_1945-12-20_print.htm; Brooks, "Interview."

71. "Memorandum of Conversation, by the Secretary of State, Bermuda, 4 December 1953," in *Foreign Relations of the United States, 1952–1954, Western European Security, Volume V, Part 2*; "United States Delegation Minutes, Bermuda, 4 December 1953," in *Foreign Relations of the United States, 1952–1954, Western European Security, Volume V, Part 2*; Moran, 471.

72. Makins, "Weekly Political Summary, 5–11 December 1953."

73. Dwight D. Eisenhower, "Address Before the General Assembly of the United Nations on Peaceful Uses of Atomic Energy, 8 December 1953." http://www.presidency.ucsb.edu/ws/?pid=9774; Moran, 459–60.

74. Eisenhower, "Address Before the General Assembly of the United Nations on Peaceful Uses of Atomic Energy, 8 December 1953."

75. John F. Dulles, "Statement by the Secretary of State of the United States at the NATO Conference in Paris, 14 December 1953." https://history.state.gov/historical documents/frus1952-54v05p1/d238.

76. Kevin Ruane, "Agonizing Reappraisals: Anthony Eden, John Foster Dulles, and the Crisis of European Defense, 1953-54," *Diplomacy and Statecraft* (13:4): 151–52; ibid., 155; ibid., 164.

77. Moran, 452; ibid., 539; ibid., 542; Colville, 684; ibid., 687.

78. Makins, "The World Since the War: The Third Phase," 5; ibid., 7–8; ibid., 13–16.

Conclusion

The Legacy of 1953 in the Early Twenty-First Century

North Korea thrived in the wake of the 1953 armistice under the leadership of Premier Kim Il Sung and with the financial aid of its Soviet and Chinese allies. Despite South Korean President Syngman Rhee's discontent with the terms of the truce, the South was unable to renew its war against the North without US support. The decreased threat of armed conflict allowed Kim's government to focus on building up the North Korean economy. By 1959, Kim Il Sung's economic programs put North Korean industrial and agricultural production far above where it had been before the Korean War. South Korea experienced its own economic boom in the 1960s. After the death of President Rhee in 1960, the South Korean government used US and Japanese financial assistance to transform the country from an agrarian society to a worldwide exporter of manufactured goods. Although the 1953 armistice prevented the Korean War from reigniting, tension between the United States and North Korea persisted. The climate remained especially volatile along the 38th Parallel, where North Korean and American military forces stood guard on either side of the demilitarized zone. A major crisis erupted in 1968 when North Korean naval vessels opened fired upon and captured the *USS Pueblo* in the Sea of Japan. It took the US government eleven months to negotiate the release of the ship's eighty-two crewmen from a North Korean prison.[1]

The predicament on the Korean Peninsula continues to be tense and complicated in the twenty-first century. North Korea's development of weapons of mass destruction in 2006 raised anxieties throughout the region and around the world. The country possesses approximately forty nuclear warheads as of 2018. Missile tests since 2013 demonstrated North Korea's potential to launch nuclear strikes against South Korea, neighboring Asian countries, and even Alaska. Meanwhile, reunification of the peninsula remains only a

The USS Pueblo is on display in Pyongyang, North Korea. North Korean naval vessels captured the Pueblo in the Sea of Japan in 1968, and the North Korean government held its crew captive for eleven months. Tension over this incident nearly reignited war between the United States and North Korea. *Credit:* Goddard_Photography.

remote possibility. Both North and South Korea desire unification, but hold very different visions of what a single Korea should look like.[2]

North Korea's weapons of mass destruction program is a chief security concern for the United States in the twenty-first century. US strategy for discouraging and disrupting North Korean nuclear weapons development includes a combination of economic sanctions, military deterrence, and cyber espionage. In addition to refusing to recognize North Korea as a sovereign nation, the United States has levied numerous sanctions against the country since 2006. These sanctions initially pertained to military supplies and luxury goods, but have expanded to include fossil fuels, raw materials, and food. The United States increased its exclusionary tactics in 2017 with travel restrictions and the freezing of North Korean financial assets associated with the United States. The United States still has a defense alliance with South Korea and maintains a military presence in and around the peninsula, with ground forces along the demilitarized zone, naval vessels in the nearby Sea of Japan, heavy bombers in Korean airspace, and intercontinental ballistic missile capabilities throughout the region. The United States outfitted South Korea with its own eight hundred million dollar high altitude antiballistic missile defense system in 2017. Cyber espionage is the United States's latest method of thwarting North Korea's weapons program. American hackers caused a nationwide internet network outage in North Korea in 2017. In the future, cyber espionage may enable the United States to steal government and military secrets from North Korea, empty its government bank accounts, and disable its missile-launch capabilities.[3]

China's relationship with North Korea ranges from providing it with vital economic support to condemning its militaristic behavior. Over eighty percent of North Korea's trade is with China, such as food, fossil fuels, and arms (including missile components). At the same time, the Chinese government discourages North Korea's weapons of mass destruction initiative and observes some of the US/UN sanctions against the country. China's complex relationship with North Korea is largely due to their conflicting national, regional, and global objectives. Despite their defense alliance, the Chinese view North Korea as a potential military rival in the Far East. The Chinese also have a vested interest in maintaining peace in Korea, as a military conflict on the Korean Peninsula would create a border security crisis for China. Security was the reason for China increasing its military presence along the North Korean border in 2017. This move drew criticism from the North Korean government. China's improved diplomatic and economic relationship with South Korea since the 1990s has also contributed to tension with its North Korean ally.[4]

The South Korean government has shown a willingness to increase diplomatic and economic interactions with the North in the twenty-first century. The North has demonstrated a similar interest, but is less enthusiastic about softening its defensive military posture in the region. North Korea considers its nuclear arsenal as essential to its national security and influence as a Far Eastern power. South Korean and US insistence upon the North's denuclearization caused a ten-year diplomatic blackout between the two nations. Prospects for negotiation improved, however, when the two Koreas declared a truce during the 2018 Winter Olympics in PyeongChang, South Korea. This prompted several meetings along the demilitarized zone between South Korean President Moon Jae-in and Supreme Leader of North Korea Kim Jong-un. A summit between US President Donald J. Trump and Supreme Leader Kim took place in Singapore in June 2018. The meeting between these heads of state was the first of its kind and resulted in a signed statement pledging both nations' commitment to preserving peace on the Korean Peninsula, denuclearization, and the sovereignty and security of both Koreas.[5] A second Trump/Kim summit in Vietnam in February 2019 was less productive than the Singapore meeting. Despite these steps toward dialogue, resolving both North and South Korea's claims as the legitimate government of Korea continues to be the biggest obstruction to permanent peace and reunification.

China's economic, industrial, and military growth in the closing decades of the twentieth century and early 2000s has become a challenge to US influence in Asia, the Pacific, and around the world. Beginning in the 1970s, the United States resigned itself to accepting China's role in the global economy by opening trade with the Chinese and encouraging US/China financial investments. The United States even supported China's admittance into the World Trade Organization (WTO) in 2001. The United States has also come to accept China's role in the diplomatic affairs of Asia and the Pacific. In recent times, the United States has been mindful of Chinese interests when formulating and conducting foreign policy throughout the region. Needless to say, this poses a particular challenge in respect to the Korean Peninsula. While the United States and China are both uneasy with North Korea's weapons of mass destruction program, they are still beholden to their regional interests and allies. One ongoing clash of interests has been over a collection of approximately 250 islands and atolls in the South China Sea. Communist China assumed dominion over these islands and the surrounding waterways in the late 1950s, but these claims conflict with those of US allies Taiwan and the Philippines. This disagreement turned dangerous in 2009 when Chinese vessels and aircraft harassed a US Navy research ship, the *USNS Impeccable*, in the South China Sea. The Chinese demanded the American vessel evacuate the area. A four-day standoff ensued and did not deescalate until a US Navy destroyer arrived to escort the *Impeccable* as it completed its survey work. Both nations considered themselves justified in their actions, and the US Navy continues to operate in the South China Sea despite China's claim over the waterway.[6]

American commentators have used the term "trade war" to refer to the economic competition between the United States and China in the twenty-first century. The United States adjusted its economic policies to reduce its trade deficit with China in 2017. These protectionist tactics included tariffs on over one thousand Chinese imports and restrictions on Chinese investments in American industry and technology. China retaliated with tariffs on over one hundred US imports, including cars, airplanes, and agricultural products. Despite the economic tension, diplomacy has produced significant coopera-tion between the two nations. President Trump visited with Chinese President Xi Jinping in April 2017. The two leaders opened several ongoing threads of discourse aimed at maintaining peace on the Korean Peninsula, resolving tension in the South China Sea, and promoting the nonproliferation of nuclear weapons. Other discussion points pertained to joint law enforcement efforts to combat black-market weapons sales and expanding cultural exchange without encroaching upon intellectual property rights.[7]

As 1953 came to a close, French General Henri Navarre amassed his forces in the fortified valley of Dien Bien Phu in northwest Vietnam. The General hoped to lure the Vietminh into a costly battle of attrition and force peace negotiations on French terms. Instead, Vietnamese General Vo Nguyen Giap directed a devastating artillery bombardment against the only French airstrip in the region in March 1954. This barrage destroyed French access to rein-forcements and resupply. The Vietminh proceeded to besiege French forces in the valley for the next two months. Over ten thousand beleaguered French troops finally surrendered in May. The cost of this defeat caused the French government to declare an end to its military intervention in Indochina. The resulting armistice provided for a divided Vietnam, with the communist Viet-minh ruling in the North and a pro-French coalition governing the South. The agreement arranged for holding a referendum to unify the country in 1956. Meanwhile, the United States established the Southeast Asia Treaty Organiza-tion (SEATO) with Australia, Great Britain, France, New Zealand, Pakistan, the Philippines, and Thailand. This American-led alliance aimed to stop the spread of communism in the Asia/Pacific region. Communist Vietcong gueril-las began an unconventional war against the South after South Vietnamese President Ngo Dinh Diem refused to hold the proposed vote on unification in 1956. The United States had less than one thousand military advisors in South Vietnam at that time. Under the provisions of the SEATO alliance, US military support for South Vietnam increased to nearly five hundred thousand troops by the late 1960s.[8] The communist North Vietnamese ultimately drove out US forces in 1973 and defeated the South two years later.

The United States's erratic distribution of economic and military aid to rival countries across the Middle East caused the Middle East Defense Organization to dissolve by the end of 1953. Iraq and Turkey formed their own Baghdad Pact alliance in 1955. Within months, Great Britain, Iran, and Pakistan joined the coalition. Egypt, Syria, and Saudi Arabia responded to the Baghdad Pact with their own defense agreement. Egyptian President Gamal Abdel Nassar's strong relationship with the Soviet Union caused the Eisenhower Administration to view the Egypt/Syria/Saudi Arabia alliance as an opening for global communism's spread to the Middle East. Despite this concern, President Eisenhower refused to align the United States with the Baghdad Pact. The president worried that an American military alliance with an Arab nation would jeopardize the United States's relationship with Israel.[9]

President Nassar ignited an international crisis when he nationalized the Suez Canal in 1956. In addition to threatening European and American access to the vital waterway, the move intensified Israel's sense of isolation among its Arab neighbors. In retaliation against Nassar, Great Britain and France secretly endorsed an Israeli invasion of Egypt's Sinai Peninsula and sent their own "neutral peace-keeping" forces into the Suez Canal Zone. In truth, the covert agreement between Great Britain, France, and Israel involved more than just liberating the Suez Canal. The plan also intended to remove Nassar from power and break Egypt's hold over the Strait of Tiran, Israel's most direct access point to the Red Sea. Much to the surprise of the British, French, and Israelis, the Eisenhower Administration condemned their military operation and worked with the UN to deescalate the situation. Without US support and under international pressure, British and French forces left the Canal Zone and the Israelis temporarily withdrew from the Sinai Peninsula.[10] Ambassador Makins attributed the American decision not to standby Great Britain to "time-honored attitudes" within the US government "about the British being colonialist, and therefore not worthy of support."[11] This incident reflects the pragmatic and unpredictable US policy in the Middle East that continues into the twenty-first century.

Most Middle Eastern countries have been involved in an ongoing military struggle with Israel since its formation in 1948. This conflict escalated when Israel captured territory from Egypt, Jordan, and Syria during the Six-Day War in 1967. Some members of the international community have referred to Israel's treatment of Arab peoples living within these conquered regions as "*apartheid.*" Meanwhile, Arab resistance to Israel's occupation of these lands has taken the form of terrorist attacks conducted by internal liberation groups, such as Hamas, and external paramilitary organizations, like Hezbollah in Lebanon. Other Middle Eastern countries, such as Iran, have provided these resistance groups with funds and weapons for decades. The United States remains a loyal supporter of Israel in the twenty-first century, but has also made significant attempts to broker peace in the region. US President Jimmy Carter first hosted the heads of state of Israel and Egypt in 1978. This summit resulted in the Camp David Accords, an official end to thirty years of war between the two countries. The agreement returned the Sinai Peninsula to Egypt and introduced the possibility of self-rule for Arabs living along the Israeli-occupied western bank of the Jordan River and the Gaza coast of the Mediterranean Sea. US President Bill Clinton organized another Arab/ Israeli summit at Camp David in 2000. This conference failed to establish autonomy for Arabs living in Israeli-controlled territories, but renewed hopes for finding a solution to the Arab/Israeli Crisis. President Trump announced US recognition of Jerusalem as the capital city of Israel in 2018. Trump's decision spawned controversy around the world, as much of the international community refuses to acknowledge the contested city of Jerusalem as Israel's capital. Instead, many countries consider Jerusalem to be an independent Arab city under Israeli military occupation. The Trump Administration's recognition of Jerusalem has called into question the sincerity of US support for Arab independence in the region.[12]

Syria's destabilization is a further example of the complex challenges faced by the United States in the Middle East in the twenty-first century. The Soviet Union's alliance with Syria in the mid-1950s seemed to confirm the Eisenhower Administration's fear of communism infiltrating the Middle East. The agreement gave the Soviets a Middle Eastern ally to counterbalance Turkey's inclusion in NATO. The Assad family came to power in Syria with Hafez al-Assad's military coup in 1970. Assad expanded Syria's relationship with the Soviet Union by permitting them to build a naval base at Tartus on Syria's Mediterranean coast. Bashar al-Assad succeeded his father as President of Syria in 2000. The Arab Spring revolt in Syria in 2011 began as an attempt to overthrow the Assad Regime, but soon degenerated into a sectarian civil war.[13] The United States provided arms to groups opposing the Assad Regime and aided Syrian forces fighting against the Islamic State, one of the United States's main adversaries in its global war on terrorism. The United States also conducted airstrikes in support of its Syrian proxies. Meanwhile, Russian President Vladimir Putin chose to honor the decades-old alliance between the Soviet Union and the Assads. Putin pledged military support for the Assad Regime and launched Russian airstrikes against the Syrian insurgents. As of 2018, the United States views Russia's military intervention in Syria as a plot to expand Russian influence in the eastern Mediterranean and condemns President Putin for inciting turmoil and violence in the Middle East.[14]

The wreckage of an Israeli tank along the border of Syria and Israel serves as a reminder of the 1967 Six-Day War between Israel and its Arab neighbors. Millions of Arabs came under Israeli rule as a result of Israel's victory and territorial gains in this war. Pressure for the creation of an independent state for Arabs living in these conquered lands has been at the heart of the Arab/Israeli Crisis for decades. *Credit:* servickuz.

It wasn't until the late 1960s when the UN finally drafted the nuclear non-proliferation agreement that President Eisenhower had advocated for in 1953. The UN's 1968 *Treaty on the Non-Proliferation of Nuclear Weapons* recognized "the devastation that would be visited upon all mankind by a nuclear war" and called for "the cessation of the nuclear arms race" and worldwide "nuclear disarmament." The pact included provisions for nations both with and without nuclear arsenals. The UN identified Great Britain, China, France, India, Israel, North Korea, Pakistan, the Soviet Union, and the United States as the countries possessing nuclear weapons at the time of the agreement. Five of these nuclear powers, Great Britain, China, France, the Soviet Union and the United States, as well as eighty-eight non-nuclear nations signed the treaty. Signers committed themselves to not "induce any non-nuclear-weapon state to manufacture or otherwise acquire nuclear weapons," allow the International Atomic Energy Agency to verify "fulfillment of its obligations," and engage in "nuclear disarmament."[15]

Iran's emergence as a nuclear power in the twenty-first century has placed the country under UN suspicion of violating the *Treaty on the Non-Proliferation of Nuclear Weapons*. UN atomic energy inspectors accused Iran of being out of compliance with the nonproliferation agreement in early 2000. These allegations resulted in UN/US sanctions on Iranian commerce, oil, and financial investments. The governments of the United States, China, France, Germany, Great Britain, and Russia met with the Iranians to arranged a *Joint Comprehensive Plan of Action* in 2015. The signers of the agreement pledged to lift sanctions against Iran in exchange for its realignment with the UN's nuclear nonproliferation regulations. The United States reneged on the *Joint Comprehensive Plan of Action* in 2018 and re-imposed sanctions on Iran after a series of Iranian-sponsored terrorist attacks against US military forces in Iraq and Syria. The Iranian government viewed the US renewal of sanctions as a hostile act in violation of an international agreement and threatened retaliation. The United States responded by increasing its naval presence in the Gulf of Oman, a critical shipping lane for Middle Eastern oil.[16] As of 2019, several hostile acts have transpired between United States and Iranian naval and air forces over the vital waterway.

Although a top-level US/Soviet summit never materialized in 1953, a four-power foreign ministers conference took place in Berlin the following year. Secretary Dulles, French Minister Georges Bidault, and British Secretary Anthony Eden met with Soviet Foreign Minister Vyacheslav Molotov in 1954. For the Eisenhower Administration, the summit affirmed the Soviet Union's unwillingness to "relax the grip on the areas of Europe that they now control." Minster Molotov also made it clear that the Soviets viewed the pending EDC alliance as a direct military threat and a "great obstacle to a solution of European problems." Molotov revealed his nation's intention to assemble a European military alliance of its own by establishing a "pact" with "Soviet satellites" and "constituent republics." Despite the tough talk, Secretary Dulles reflected positively on the Berlin summit and believed the conference "provided an opportunity for the United States delegation to learn a great deal by direct contact." For example, Dulles and Molotov informally agreed that both the United States and Soviet Union favored atomic weapons regulation and wanted "to get this matter before the UN Disarmament Commission" as soon as possible.[17] After the Berlin summit, high-level meetings between the United States and Soviet Union increased over the next three decades and played a significant role in averting a disastrous conflict between the two superpowers during the Cold War. Over twenty United States/Soviet head-of-state summits took place between 1955 and 1991.

The French parliament voted against joining the EDC in 1954. The French were uncomfortable with West Germany's rearmament in the wake of two world wars and viewed the alliance as an encroachment upon their freedom to make independent military decisions. Ambassador Makins explained France's concerns about a rearmed Germany in a post-WWII, "Among many countries on the Continent, there was . . . a dilemma between the emotional antagonism toward Germany resulting from the war on one hand, and . . . the realization that Germany had to be brought into the European community."[18] The EDC became a dead issue without French participation. Meanwhile, the Soviet Union's formation of the Warsaw Pact alliance in 1955 forced the United States to increase its military presence in Europe. Just as Minister Molotov had warned at the foreign ministers conference in Berlin in 1954, the Warsaw Pact was the Soviet Union's direct response to NATO. The Soviet military alliance included Albania, Bulgaria, Czechoslovakia, East Germany, Hungary, Poland, and Romania. It asserted that "the North Atlantic bloc . . . increases the threat of another war and creates a menace to the national security of the peace-loving states." The Warsaw Pact, like NATO, claimed to be in accordance with the principles of the UN in promoting "cooperation" and the peaceful settlement of "international disputes." The alliance also included a statement of commitment to "a general reduction of armaments and prohibition of atomic, hydrogen, and other weapons of mass destruction."[19] Forty years after the Great War, the world once again found itself in the throes of a sensitive balance-of-power between two alliances depending upon military deterrence to prevent a catastrophic total war.

Russian intervention in the Ukrainian Civil War in the twenty-first century has brought the relationship between NATO and Russia to an all-time low since the Cold War. Crimea voted to secede from Ukraine and join the Russian Federation in 2014. The Russian government quickly approved the annexation, as the Crimean port city of Sevastopol has been home to Russia's Black Sea Fleet for nearly three hundred years. NATO, however, refused to recognize neither Crimea's secession from Ukraine nor Russia's annexation of the peninsula. A civil war erupted in eastern Ukraine later that year. Pro-Russian, separatist, paramilitary forces seeking to create a "New Russia" in eastern Ukraine clashed with Ukrainian anti-separatist militia. President Putin sent support to the Pro-Russian separatists in the form of "aid convoys" across the Russo/Ukrainian border. NATO suspected these vehicles of carrying military aid to the separatists and demanded Russia put a stop to the convoys. When Putin refused to halt his "aid convoys," the United States and other NATO members placed sanctions on Russian banking and investments.[20]

The United States's reassessment of its role in NATO in the twenty-first century looms ominously over the Ukrainian crisis. Many American politicians have questioned the necessity of NATO since the collapse of the Soviet Union and the Warsaw Pact in 1991. President Trump reduced US funding for NATO in 2018 and threatened to withdraw from the alliance if other members continued to neglect their financial commitment to the alliance. Only five of NATO's twenty-nine members fulfilled their financial obligation, two percent of their gross domestic product, in 2018. Meanwhile, the United States accounts for nearly half of NATO's funding. The United States has also criticized those NATO members who choose not observe US sanctions against North Korea, Iran, and Russia.[21]

Armed conflict between NATO and Russia over eastern Ukraine remains unlikely as of 2019. Ukraine is not an official NATO ally; and, without a conventional Russian military invasion of Ukraine, the civil war there remains an internal matter. Nevertheless, President Putin has been very clear in asserting that any NATO incursion into the Black Sea region will be construed as a direct threat to the Russian Federation.[22] Although NATO forces are well positioned to take military action against Russia in Europe, its members are not likely to agree on a course of action that would ignite the type of East/West conflict they managed to prevent for nearly fifty years during the Cold War.

NOTES

1. Yong-Pyo Hong, "North Korea in the 1950s: The Post Korean War Policies and their Implications," *The Korean Journal of International Relations* (Volume 44, Number, 5, 2004): 218; ibid., 222.

2. Leif-Eric Easley, "From Strategic Patience to Strategic Uncertainty: Trump, North Korea, and South Korea's New President," *World Affairs* (Summer 2017): 9; ibid., 17–18; Robert Vandemeulebroucke, "Alleviating International Tensions on the Korean Peninsula-A Blueprint," *International Journal on World Peace* (December

2017): 86; ibid., 88; Quanyi Zhang, "Commentaries on Korean Unification: Wide-Ranging Views on Korean Unification," *International Journal on World Peace* (September 2016): 71.

3. Easley, 9–12; Vandemeulebroucke, 86–87; Zhang, 71; ibid., 73; ibid., 75; Walter Lohman, "Year One of the Trump Administration's Policy: Uncertainty and Continuity," *Southeast Asian Affairs* (Volume 2018): 47.

4. Easley, 14–15; Zhang, 72; ibid., 74–77; Ian Bremmer, "As the Koreans Share an Olympic Moment, Trump Risks Irrelevance," *Time* (February 19, 2018): 6.

5. Easley, 24; Zhang, 72; Vandemeulebroucke, 88; Bremmer, 5–6.

6. Evan A. Feigenbaum, "Trump and China," *The National Interest* (January/February 2017): 42–43; Kacie Miura and Jessica Chen Weiss, "Will China Test Trump? Lessons from Past Campaigns and Elections," *The Washington Quarterly* (Winter 2017): 7; ibid., 10; Lohman, 45.

7. Randall Schweller, "Three Cheers for Trump's Foreign Policy: What the Establishment Misses," *Foreign Affairs* (September/October): 136; ibid., 138; Charles W. Calomiris, "Bluster Notwithstanding, China's Bargaining Position Will Weaken," *Cato Journal* (Spring/Summer 2018): 531; ibid., 535; Loman 45.

8. Goscha, "First Indochina War (1945–1954)," 78–79; Ruane, "Agonizing Reappraisals," 169.

9. Ruane, "Anglo-American Relations," 7; ibid., 10; ibid., 13.

10. Ahron Bregman, "Arab-Israeli Conflict," in *Twentieth-Century War and Conflict: A Concise Encyclopedia*, edited by Gordon Martel (West Sussex, UK: John Wiley and Sons, Ltd., 2015), 12.

11. Wilson, "Interview."

12. Daniel C. Kurtzer, "Choices Facing the United States: Greater Israel or Global Israel?," *Israel Studies* (23:3 Fall 2018), 246–47; ibid., 249; Daniel Byman, "Approximating War," *The National Interest* (September/October 2018), 13; ibid., 18; Ziad Abu Zayyad, "President Trump's Decision on Jerusalem Lacks International Legitimacy and Strategic Vision," *Palestine-Israel Journal* (22/23:4/1), 4–6.

13. Neil Quilliam, "Syria: The Rise of the Assads," *BBC News* (4 November 2015), http://www.bbc.com/news/world-middle-east-34709235; Lynch, 121.

14. Jonathan Marcus, "Syria Crisis: Russia's Strategy and Endgame?," *BBC News* (8 October 2015), http://www.bbc.com/news/world-europe-34474362); Lynch 122–23; Byman, 17–18.

15. United Nations Office for Disarmament Affairs. "Treaty on the Non-Proliferation of Nuclear Weapon, 1 July 1968." https://www.un.org/disarmament /wmd/nuclear/npt/text.

16. Kurtzer, 247; "Joint Comprehensive Plan of Action, 14 July 2015." https:// www.state.gov/documents/organization/245317.pdf; Byman, 18; Marc Lynch, "The New Arab Order: Power and Violence in Today's Middle East," *Foreign Affairs* (September/October 2018), 118.

17. "Memorandum of Discussion at the 186th Meeting of the National Security Council, 26 February 1954," in *Foreign Relations of the United States, 1952–1954, Germany and Austria, Volume VII, Part 1.* https://history.state.gov/historicaldocu ments/frus1952-54v07p1/d529.

18. Brooks, "Interview."

19. "Warsaw Pact, 1 May 1955." http://chnm.gmu.edu/1989/archive/files/The%20 Warsaw%20Pact_d7223aede6.pdf.

20. Vladimir Putin, "Address by President of the Russian Federation, 18 March 2014." http://en.kremlin.ru/events/president/news/20603; NATO, "Wales Summit Declaration, 5 September 2014." http://www.nato.int/cps/en/natohq/official _texts_112964.htm; Byman, 10; ibid., 13.

21. Schweller, 134; ibid., 140–41.

22. Vladimir Putin, "Federal Security Service Board Meeting, 26 March 2015." http://en.kremlin.ru/events/president/news/49006.

Bibliography

PRIMARY SOURCES

Colville, John. *The Fringes of Power: 10 Downing Street Diaries, 1939–1955.* London: W.W. Norton and Co., 1985.

Duncan, David Douglas. "The Year of the Snake: A Time of Fear and Worry Comes Over Warring Indochina." *Life* (August 3, 1953): 73–91.

Editorial. "Indochina, France, and the US." *Life* (August 3, 1953): 28.

Lord Moran. *Churchill: Taken from the Diaries of Lord Moran.* Boston, MA: Houghton Mifflin Co., 1966.

Makins, Roger. "The World Since the War: The Third Phase." *Foreign Affairs* (33:1 October 1954): 1–16.

———. "Weekly Political Summary, 5–11 December 1953."

———. "Weekly Political Summary, 31 October–7 November 1953."

———. "Weekly Political Summary, 24–30 October 1953."

———. "Weekly Political Summary, 17–23 October 1953."

———. "Weekly Political Summary, 10–16 October 1953."

———. "Weekly Political Summary, 3–9 October 1953."

———. "Weekly Political Summary, 25 September–2 October 1953."

———. "Weekly Political Summary, 12–18 September 1953."

———. "Weekly Political Summary, 5–11 September 1953."

———. "Weekly Political Summary, 28 August–4 September 1953."

———. "Weekly Political Summary, 15–21 August 1953."

———. "Weekly Political Summary, 8–14 August 1953."

———. "Weekly Political Summary, 1–7 August 1953."

———. "Weekly Political Summary, 25–31 July 1953."

———. "Weekly Political Summary, 11–17 July 1953."

———. "Weekly Political Summary, 4–10 July 1953."

———. "Weekly Political Summary, 27 June–3 July 1953."

———. "Weekly Political Summary, 20–26 June 1953."

————. "Weekly Political Summary, 13–19 June 1953."

————. "Weekly Political Summary, 6–12 June 1953."

————. "Weekly Political Summary, 30 May–5 June 1953."

————. "Weekly Political Summary, 23–29 May 1953."

————. "Weekly Political Summary, 16–22 May 1953."

————. "Weekly Political Summary, 9–15 May 1953."

————. "Weekly Political Summary, 2–8 May 1953."

————. "Weekly Political Summary, 25 April–1 May 1953."

————. "Weekly Political Summary, 18–24 April 1953."

————. "Weekly Political Summary, 11–17 April 1953."

————. "Weekly Political Summary, 4–10 April 1953."

————. "Weekly Political Summary, 28 March–3 April 1953."

————. "Weekly Political Summary, 21–27 March 1953."

————. "Weekly Political Summary, 14–20 March 1953."

————. "Weekly Political Summary, 7–13 March 1953."

————. "Weekly Political Summary, 28 February–6 March 1953.

————. "Weekly Political Summary, 21–27 February 1953."

————. "Weekly Political Summary, 14–20 February 1953."

————. "Weekly Political Summary, 7–13 February 1953."

————. "Weekly Political Summary, 24–30 January 1953."

————. "Weekly Political Summary, 17–23 January 1953."

————. "Weekly Political Summary, 10–16 January 1953."

————. "Weekly Political Summary, 3–9 January 1953."

ONLINE DOCUMENTS

"ANZUS Treaty, 1 September 1951." Accessed October 4, 2017. http://avalon.law yale.edu/20th_century/usmu002.asp.

"Armistice Agreement for the Restoration of the South Korean State, 27 July 1953." Accessed October 13, 2017. https://www.ourdocuments.gov/doc.php?flash=true& doc=85&page=transcript.

"Atomic Energy Act, 22 April 1946." Accessed July 30, 2019. http://www.nuclearfiles .org/menu/library/treaties/atomic-energy-act/trty_atomic-energy-act_1945-12-20 _print.htm.

Attlee, Clement R. "Foreign Affairs, House of Commons, 12 May 1953." Accessed October 23, 2017. http://hansard.millbanksystems.com/commons/1953/may/12 /foreign-affairs#S5CV0515P0_19530512_HOC_263.

Brooks, Philip C. "Oral History Interview with Sir Roger Makins, 15 June 1964." Accessed July 30, 2019. https://www.trumanlibrary.gov/library/oral-histories/makinsr.

Central Intelligence Agency. "Reaction to Malenkov's Speech of 8 August 1953," 14 August 1953. Accessed October 25, 2017. https://www.cia.gov/library/reading room/docs/CIA-RDP82-00046R000200050004-0.pdf.

————. "Comment on Egyptian Situation," July 13, 1953. Accessed January 26, 2018. https://www.cia.gov/library/readingroom/docs/CIA-RDP91T01172R000 200320012-3.pdf.

————. "Summary of *Pravda's* reply to President Eisenhower's Address of 16 April," April 25, 1953. Accessed October 25, 2017. https://www.cia.gov/library /readingroom/docs/CIARDP91T01172R000200290051-4.pdf.

Churchill, Winston S. "Foreign Affairs, House of Commons, 11 May 1953." Accessed October 23, 2017. http://hansard.millbanksystems.com/commons/1953/may/11 /foreign-affairs#column_883.

————. "Iron Curtain Speech, 5 March 1946." Accessed April 3, 2018. https:// sourcebooks.fordham.edu/mod/churchill-iron.asp.

"Churchill's Masterly Review." *The Advertiser*, October 12, 1953. Accessed June 13, 2018. https://trove.nla.gov.au/newspaper/article/48935940.

Dulles, John F. "Statement by the Secretary of State of the United States at the NATO Conference in Paris, 14 December 1953." Accessed March 27, 2017. https://history .state.gov/historicaldocuments/frus1952-54v05p1/d238.

————. "Address to the United Nations, 17 September 1953." Accessed October 13, 2017.

————. "Korean Problems, 2 September 1953." Accessed October 13, 2017. https:// history.state.gov/historicaldocuments/frus1952-54v13p1/d385.

————. "US Constitution and UN Charter: An Appraisal, 26 August 1953." Accessed May 31, 2018. https://babel.hathitrust.org/cgi/pt?id=umn.31951d03563129p.

————. "Report on the Near East, 1 June 1953." Accessed January 24, 2018. https:// archive.org/details/ldpd_10987272_000.

————. "Statement on Liberation Policy, 15 January 1953." Accessed April 6, 2018. http://teachingamericanhistory.org/library/document/statement-on-liberation -policy/.

Eisenhower, Dwight D. "Address Before the General Assembly of the United Nations on Peaceful Uses of Atomic Energy, 8 December 1953." Accessed March 27, 2017. http://www.presidency.ucsb.edu/ws/?pid=9774.

————. "News Conference, 4 November 1953." Accessed April 3, 2018. http://www .presidency.ucsb.edu/ws/index.php?pid=9754.

————. "Address at the Sixth National Assembly of the United Church Women, Atlantic City, New Jersey, 6 October 1953." Accessed March 27, 2017. http://www .presidency.ucsb.edu/ws/index.php?pid=9718.

————. "Remarks at the Governors' Conference, Seattle, Washington, 4 August 1953." Accessed January 30, 2018. http://www.presidency.ucsb.edu/ws/?pid=9663.

————. "News Conference, 28 May 1953." Accessed October 30, 2017. http://www .presidency.ucsb.edu/ws/index.php?pid=9860.

————. "Chance for Peace Address, 16 April 1953." Accessed October 13, 2017. https://www.eisenhower.archives.gov/all_about_ike/speeches/chance_for_peace .pdf.

————. "News Conference, 25 February 1953." Accessed March 23, 2018. http:// www.presidency.ucsb.edu/ws/index.php?pid=9656.

————. "News Conference, 17 February 1953." Accessed October 13, 2017. http://www.presidency.ucsb.edu/ws/index.php?pid=9623.

————. "Annual Message to the Congress on the State of the Union, 2 February 1953." Accessed January 11, 2018. http://www.presidency.ucsb.edu/ws/?pid=9829.

————. "Inaugural Address, 20 January 1953." Accessed October 12, 2017. http://www.presidency.ucsb.edu/ws/?pid=9600.

House of Commons. "Sudan (Anglo-Egyptian Agreement)." Accessed October 4, 2017. http://hansard.millbanksystems.com/commons/1953/feb/12/sudan-anglo-egyptian-agreement.

"Joint Comprehensive Plan of Action, 14 July 2015." Accessed November 7, 2018. https://www.state.gov/documents/organization/245317.pdf.

Marshall, George C. "Marshall Plan Speech, Harvard University, 5 June 1947." Accessed July 30, 2019. https://www.marshallfoundation.org/marshall/the-marshall-plan/marshall-plan-speech/.

"Memorandum of Conversation, by the Secretary of State, Bermuda, December 4, 1953." In *Foreign Relations of the United States, 1952-1954, Western European Security, Volume V, Part 2*. Accessed October 13, 2017. https://history.state.gov/historicaldocuments/frus1952-54v05p2/d336.

"Memorandum of Discussion at the 186th Meeting of the National Security Council, 26 February 1954." In *Foreign Relations of the United States, 1952–1954, Germany and Austria, Volume VII, Part 1*. Accessed April 4, 2018. https://history.state.gov/historicaldocuments/frus1952-54v07p1/d529.

"Military Facilities in Spain: Agreement between the United States and Spain, September 26, 1953." Accessed April 3, 2018. http://avalon.law.yale.edu/20th_century/sp1953.asp.

"North Atlantic Treaty, 4 April 1949." Accessed July 17, 2018. https://www.nato.int/cps/ie/natohq/official_texts_17120.htm.

NATO, "Wales Summit Declaration, 5 September 2014." Accessed November 30, 2018. http://www.nato.int/cps/en/natohq/official_texts_112964.htm.

Putin, Vladimir. "Federal Security Service Board Meeting, 26 March 2015." Accessed November 30, 2018. http://en.kremlin.ru/events/president/news/49006.

————. "Address by President of the Russian Federation, 18 March 2014." Accessed November 30, 2018. http://en.kremlin.ru/events/president/news/20603.

Smith, Trevor. "Churchill's Great Comeback." *The Advertiser*, 12 October 1953. Accessed June 13, 2018. https://trove.nla.gov.au/newspaper/article/48935702.

"Treaty of Dunkirk, 4 March 1947." Accessed July 30, 2019. https://alphahistory.com/coldwar/treaty-of-dunkirk-1947/.

"Tripartite Declaration, 25 May 1950." Accessed October 4, 2017. http://www.jewishvirtuallibrary.org/tripartite-declaration-may-1950.

Truman, Harry S. "Farewell Address to the American People, 15 January 1953." Accessed October 12, 2017. http://www.presidency.ucsb.edu/ws/index.php?pid=14392.

————. "Address before a Joint Session of Congress, 12 March 1947." Accessed April 2, 2018. http://avalon.law.yale.edu/20th_century/trudoc.asp.

United Nations Office for Disarmament Affairs. "Treaty on the Non-Proliferation of Nuclear Weapon, 1 July 1968." Accessed July 17, 2018. https://www.un.org /disarmament/wmd/nuclear/npt/text.

"United States Delegation Minutes, Bermuda, Undated." In *Foreign Relations of the United States, 1952-1954, Western European Security, Volume V, Part 2.* Accessed October 13, 2017. https://history.state.gov/historicaldocuments/frus1952-54v05p2 /d353.

"United States Delegation Minutes, Bermuda, 4 December 1953." In *Foreign Relations of the United States, 1952-1954, Western European Security, Volume V, Part 2.* Accessed October 13, 2017. https://history.state.gov/historicaldocuments /frus1952-54v05p2/d341.

"Warsaw Pact, 1 May 1955." Accessed August 1, 2018. http://chnm.gmu.edu/1989 /archive/files/The%20Warsaw%20Pact_d7223aede6.pdf.

Wilson, Theodore A. "Oral History Interview with Sir Roger Makins, 10 August 1970." Accessed July 30, 2019. https://www.trumanlibrary.gov/library/oral-histories /makinsr2.

BOOKS

Bjorge, Gary J. "Chinese Civil War (Modern)." In *Twentieth-Century War and Conflict: A Concise Encyclopedia*, edited by Gordon Martel 53-57. West Sussex, UK: John Wiley and Sons, Ltd., 2015.

Bregman, Ahron. "Arab-Israeli Conflict." In *Twentieth-Century War and Conflict: A Concise Encyclopedia*, edited by Gordon Martel 53–57. West Sussex, UK: John Wiley and Sons, Ltd., 2015.

Farrell, Brian P. "Malayan Emergency (1948–1960)." In *Twentieth-Century War and Conflict: A Concise Encyclopedia*, edited by Gordon Martel 53-57. West Sussex, UK: John Wiley and Sons, Ltd., 2015.

Goscha, Christopher E. "First Indochina War (1945–1954)." In *Twentieth-Century War and Conflict: A Concise Encyclopedia*, edited by Gordon Martel 53–57. West Sussex, UK: John Wiley and Sons, Ltd., 2015.

Lee, Steven H. "Korean War (1949–1953)." In *Twentieth-Century War and Conflict: A Concise Encyclopedia*, edited by Gordon Martel 115–21. West Sussex, UK: John Wiley and Sons, Ltd., 2015.

Lookingbill, Brad D. *The American Military: A Narrative History.* West Sussex, UK: John Wiley and Sons, Ltd., 2013.

Wevill, Richard. *Diplomacy, Roger Makins, and the Anglo-American Relationship.* Burlington, VT: Ashgate, 2014.

ARTICLES

Abu Zayyad, Ziad. "President Trump's Decision on Jerusalem Lacks International Legitimacy and Strategic Vision." *Palestine-Israel Journal* (22/23:4/1): 4–6.

Boler, David. "Bermuda: Model for Summits to Come." *Finest Hour: Journal of the Churchill Center* (Spring 2003): 14–15.

Bremmer, Ian. "As the Koreas Share an Olympic Moment, Trump Risks Irrelevance." *Time* (February 19, 2018): 5–6.

Byman, Daniel. "Approximating War." *The National Interest* (September/October 2018): 10–19.

Calomiris, Charles W. "Bluster Notwithstanding, China's Bargaining Position Will Weaken." *Cato Journal* (Spring/Summer 2018): 531–36.

Easley, Leif-Eric. "From Strategic Patience to Strategic Uncertainty: Trump, North Korea, and South Korea's New President." *World Affairs* (Summer 2017): 7–31.

Feigenbaum, Evan A. "Trump and China." *The National Interest* (January/February 2017): 35–45.

Hong, Yong-Pyo. "North Korea in the 1950s: The Post Korean War Policies and their Implications." *The Korean Journal of International Relations* (Volume 44, Number 5, 2004): 215–34.

Kelly, Saul. "Transatlantic Diplomat: Sir Roger Makins, Ambassador to Washington and Joint Permanent Secretary to the Treasury." *Contemporary British History* (Volume 13, Number 2, 1999): 157–77.

Kurtzer, Daniel C. "Choices Facing the United States: Greater Israel or Global Israel?" *Israel Studies* (23:3 Fall 2018): 246–52.

Lohman, Walter. "Year One of the Trump Administration's Policy: Uncertainty and Continuity." *Southeast Asian Affairs* (Volume 2018): 43–58.

Lynch, Marc. "The New Arab Order: Power and Violence in Today's Middle East." *Foreign Affairs* (September/October 2018): 116–24.

Marcus, Jonathan. "Syria Crisis: Russia's Strategy and Endgame?" *BBC News* (October 8, 2015.) Accessed November 6, 2018. http://www.bbc.com/news/world -europe-34474362.

Miura, Kacie and Jessica Chen Weiss. "Will China Test Trump? Lessons from Past Campaigns and Elections." *The Washington Quarterly* (Winter 2017): 7–25.

Quilliam, Neil. "Syria: The Rise of the Assads." *BBC News* (November 4, 2015.) Accessed 6 November 2018. http://www.bbc.com/news/world-middle -east-34709235.

Ruane, Kevin. "Anglo-American Relations: The Cold War and Middle East Defense, 1953–1955." *Journal of Transatlantic Studies* (4:1 2006): 1–25.

Ruane, Kevin. "Agonizing Reappraisals: Anthony Eden, John Foster Dulles, and the Crisis of European Defense, 1953–54." *Diplomacy and Statecraft* (13:4): 151–85.

Schweller, Randall. "Three Cheers for Trump's Foreign Policy: What the Establishment Misses." *Foreign Affairs* (September/October): 133–43.

Vandemeulebroucke, Robert. "Alleviating International Tensions on the Korean Peninsula-A Blueprint." *International Journal of World Peace* (December 2017): 86–89.

Zhang, Quanyi. "Commentaries on Korean Unification: Wide-Ranging Views on Korean Unification." *International Journal on World Peace* (September 2016): 71–79.

Index

About the Author

Jeffrey LaMonica is an associate professor of history and coordinator of the global studies program at Delaware County Community College in Media, Pennsylvania. He holds an MPhil. in global studies from the University of Pennsylvania, an MA in modern European history from Villanova University, and a BA in history from LaSalle University. Jeffrey resides in Philadelphia.